ACTORS

The MIT Press Series in Artificial Intelligence
Edited by Patrick Henry Winston and Michael Brady

Artificial Intelligence: An MIT Perspective, Volume I: Expert Problem Solving, Natural Language Understanding, Intelligent Computer Coaches, Representation and Learning edited by Patrick Henry Winston and Richard Henry Brown, 1979

Artificial Intelligence: An MIT Perspective, Volume II: Understanding Vision, Manipulation, Computer Design, Symbol Manipulation edited by Patrick Henry Winston and Richard Henry Brown, 1979

NETL: A System for Representing and Using Real-World Knowledge by Scott Fahlman, 1979

The Interpretation of Visual Motion by Shimon Ullman, 1979

A Theory of Syntactic Recognition for Natural Language by Mitchell P. Marcus, 1980

Turtle Geometry: The Computer as a Medium for Exploring Mathematics by Harold Abelson and Andrea diSessa, 1981

From Images to Surfaces: A Computational Study of the Human Early Visual System by William Eric Leifur Grimson, 1981

Robot Manipulators: Mathematics, Programming and Control by Richard P. Paul, 1981

Computational Models of Discourse edited by Michael Brady and Robert C. Berwick, 1982

Robot Motion: Planning and Control by Michael Brady, John M. Hollerbach, Timothy Johnson, Tomas Lozano-Pèrez, and Matthew Mason, 1982

In-Depth Understanding: A Computer Model of Integrated Processing for Narrative Comprehension by Michael G. Dyer, 1983

Robotics Research: The First International Symposium edited by Michael Brady and Richard Paul, 1984

Robotics Research: The Second International Symposium edited by Hideo Hanafusa and Hirochika Inoue, 1985

Robot Hands and the Mechanics of Manipulation by Matthew T. Mason and J. Kenneth Salisbury, Jr., 1985

Legged Robots that Balance by Marc Raibert, 1985

The Acquisition of Syntactic Knowledge by Robert C. Berwick, 1985

The Connection Machine by W. Daniel Hillis, 1985

Object Oriented Concurrent Programming by Akinori Yonezawa and Mario Tokoro, 1986

Machine Interpretation of Line Drawings by Kokichi Sugihara, 1986

Knowledge Based Tutoring: The GUIDON Program by William Clancey, 1986

ACTORS: A Model of Concurrent Computation in Distributed Systems by Gul A. Agha, 1986

Peter Denning, consulting editor, computer science books

ACTORS:
A Model of Concurrent Computation
in Distributed Systems

Gul A. Agha

The MIT Press
Cambridge, Massachusetts
London, England

PUBLISHER'S NOTE
This format is intended to reduce the cost of publishing certain works in book form and to shorten the gap between editorial preparation and final publication. Detailed editing and composition have been avoided by photographing the text of this book directly from the author's prepared copy.

This book was printed and bound in the United States of America.

Library of Congress Cataloging-in-Publication Data

Agha, Gul A.
  Actors : a model of concurrent computation in distributed systems.

  (The MIT Press series in artificial intelligence)
  Bibliography: p.
  Includes index.
  1. Electronic data processing—Distributed processing.   2. Parallel processing (Electronic computers)   I. Title.   II. Series.
  QA76.9.D5A37   1986   004'.36   86-21408
  ISBN 0-262-01092-5

To All Sentient Life

In Memory Of

Sachal

(Aug 1983 – May 1984)

Contents

List of Figures

Series Foreword

Artificial intelligence is the study of intelligence using the ideas and methods of computation. Unfortunately, a definition of intelligence seems impossible at the moment because intelligence appears to be an amalgam of so many information-processing and information-representation abilities.

Of course psychology, philosophy, linguistics, and related disciplines offer various perspectives and methodologies for studying intelligence. For the most part, however, the theories proposed in these fields are too incomplete and too vaguely stated to be realized in computational terms. Something more is needed, even though valuable ideas, relationships, and constraints can be gleaned from traditional studies of what are, after all, impressive existence proofs that intelligence is in fact possible.

Artificial intelligence offers a new perspective and a new methodology. Its central goal is to make computers intelligent, both to make them more useful and to understand the principles that make intelligence possible. That intelligent computers will be extremely useful is obvious. The more profound point is that artificial intelligence aims to understand intelligence using the ideas and methods of computation, thus offering a radically new and different basis for theory formation. Most of the people doing artificial intelligence believe that these theories will apply to any intelligent information processor, whether biological or solid state.

There are side effects that deserve attention, too. Any program that will successfully model even a small part of intelligence will be inherently massive and complex. Consequently, artificial intelligence continually confronts the limits of computer science technology. The problems encountered have been hard enough and interesting enough to seduce artificial intelligence people into working on them with enthusiasm. It is natural, then, that there has been a steady flow of ideas from artificial intelligence to computer science, and the flow shows no sign of abating.

The purpose of this MIT Press Series in Artificial Intelligence is to provide people in many areas, both professionals and students, with timely, detailed information about what is happening on the frontiers in research centers all over the world.

Patrick Henry Winston
Michael Brady

Preface

It is generally believed that the next generation of computers will involve massively parallel architectures. This thesis studies one of the proposed paradigms for exploiting parallelism, namely the actor model of concurrent computation. It is our contention that the actor model provides a general framework in which computation in distributed parallel systems can be exploited. The scope of this thesis is generally limited to theoretical and programming language aspects of the model, as opposed to specific implementation or application issues.

Many observers have noted the computational power that is likely to become available with the advent of a new generation of computers. This work makes a small contribution in the direction of realizing technology which seems just on the horizon. The possibilities that emerge from the availability of a massive increase in computational power are simply mind boggling. Unfortunately, humankind has generally lacked the foresight to use the resources that science has provided in a manner that would be compatible with its long-term survival. Somehow we have to develop an ethic that values compassion rather than consumption, to acquire a reverence for life itself. Otherwise this work, among others, will be another small step in the global march towards self-destruction.

The research reported in this book was carried out for the most part at M.I.T., where I have been working with the *Message-Passing Semantics Group*. The group is currently implementing the *Apiary architecture* for *Open Systems*, which is based on the actor model. Much of the development of the actor paradigm has been inspired by the work of Carl Hewitt whose encouragement and constructive criticism has been indispensable to the development of the ideas in this thesis.

This thesis has been influenced by other work in the area of concurrency, most notably that of Robin Milner. Although I have shied away from using a λ-calculus like notation for an actor calculus, the transition system developed has a similar flavor. A programming language notation is used for purposes of overall clarity in expressing simple programs.

John Holland has provided both intellectual impetus and moral support over the years; in particular, numerous useful discussions with John have led to a better perspective on ideas in the field. I am also indebted to William Rounds for numerous suggestions, among them to develop a simple actor language and to illustrate its flavor by treating a number of commonly understood examples. My first thorough exposure to object-oriented programming languages was in a course offered by Paul Scott. Conversations with Robin Milner, Vaughn Pratt, and Joe Stoy have provided important feedback. Will Clinger's thesis interested me in the area of actor semantics. Members of the Message-Passing Semantics Group at M.I.T. have created an atmosphere which made the work described here possible. In particular, Johnathan Amsterdam, Peter de Jong, Henry Lieberman, Carl Manning, Chunka Mui and Thomas Reinhardt provided helpful comments. Carl Manning, Thomas Reinhardt, and Toon K. Wong also read drafts of this book. Needless to add, I am solely responsible for any remaining errors.

The work described in here was made possible by generous funding from the System Development Foundation and by the support of the Artificial Intelligence Laboratory at M.I.T. The book is a revised version of a doctoral dissertation submitted to the University of Michigan, Ann Arbor. John Holland and Carl Hewitt served as Co-chairs of the dissertation committee and William Rounds, Paul Scott and Andreas Blass were members. Each of them provided significant comments on the work.

Finally, the time during which the ideas in this thesis were developed was a rather intense time in the lives of my family. Nothing would have been possible without the patient cooperation of my wonderful wife Jennifer Cole. It must be added that it was only due to the high spirits maintained by our son Sachal through most of his short, difficult life that any work at all could have been done by me.

Gul Agha
Cambridge, Massachusetts
July 1986.

ACTORS

Chapter 1

Introduction

The purpose of a language is to communicate; that of a programming language is to communicate to a computer the actions it ought to perform. There are two different sorts of objectives one can emphasize in the design of a programming language: *efficiency* in execution, and *expressiveness*. By "efficiency," we refer here only to the speed with which the actions implied in a program can be carried out by the computer. In a precise sense the most efficient programming language would be one that literally told the computer what actions to carry out; in other words, a machine language.[1] Expressiveness refers to the ease with which a program can be understood and shown to behave correctly. A programming language is expressive to the extent that it can be used to specify reasonable behaviors in the simplest possible terms.

A programming language that maximized efficiency would not necessarily lead to the specification of programs with the best *performance*. This is simply because the programmer may end up spending more time figuring out *how* to express rather than *what* to express. The best gains in performance are to be achieved by discovering less computationally complex methods of achieving the same result.

The goal of introducing new programming languages has generally been to make it simpler to express more complex behavior. The class of actions computers were first expected to carry out was that of computing well-defined mathematical functions. However, such computations are no longer the only tasks a modern computer performs. The storage of information, sorting and searching through such information, and even exploration in real-time of an imprecisely defined domain have emerged as significant

---

[1] Of course every kind of processor has its own machine language. Some of these languages may be "inherently" more efficient than others.

applications. For example, computerized *databases*, such as the records maintained by a state Motor Vehicles Bureau, and *artificial intelligence* applications, such as computerized vehicles pioneering the navigation of the Martian surface, are some uses of the computer. This more general use of computer programs has, in and of itself, important consequences for the class of behaviors we are interested in expressing.

Although newer programming languages have generally favored considerations of expressiveness over those of efficiency, the ability to solve complex problems by means of the computer has nevertheless increased. This remarkable trend has been achieved by creating faster and bigger processors. However, there is now good reason to believe that we may have approached the point of diminishing returns in terms of the size and speed of the individual processor. Smaller processors would already be far more cost-effective, if we could use large numbers of them cooperatively. One precondition for cooperative computing is the ability to use processors in parallel.

This brings us to the central topic of consideration in this book; namely, the development of a suitable language for *concurrency*. By concurrency we mean the *potentially* parallel execution of desired actions. Actually, concurrency by itself is not the real issue—after all concurrency has been exploited for a long time in the software revolution caused by time-sharing. The key difference between the now classic problem of operating systems, and our desire to exploit concurrency in the context of cooperative computing, is that in the former there is little interaction between the various "jobs" or "processes" that are executed concurrently. Indeed, the correctness of an operating system is dependent on making sure that none of the numerous (user-defined) processes affect each other.

Our problem is quite the reverse: we wish to have a number of processes work together in a meaningful manner. This doesn't really imply that there are no important lessons to be learned from operating system theory. For example, notice that we switched from talking about "processors" to talking in terms of "processes." A *processor* is a physical machine while a *process* is an abstract computation. From operating systems we know that we may improve over-all performance of a processor by executing several processes concurrently instead of sequentially. How the processors are utilized is an issue for the underlying *network architecture* supporting the language. Our interest is in a model that exploits concurrently executed processes without making specific assumptions about their concrete realization in terms of a particular configuration on a network of processors. In general, the processes may be distributed over a network of processors which can be used in parallel; however, if a programming language did *not* support concurrency, such a distributed architecture would not result in any improvement in performance over a single processor.

Actually, we are not so much concerned with a particular programming language, but rather, with the meta-linguistic issues behind the constructs of a concurrent language. The operational semantics of a language defines an instruction set for computation on an *abstract machine*. (More precisely, in case of the actor model, a system of machines). We are interested in the characteristics of the underlying models of computation. Specifically, we will examine the issues of expressiveness and efficiency in the context of concurrent computation.

There are some intrinsic reasons for a theory of concurrency as well. One of these is the relevance of concurrency to an understanding of intelligent systems and communities. In particular, natural systems that appear to learn or adapt are all intrinsically parallel, and in fact quite massively so: the brain of animals, ecological communities, social organizations whether these are of human or non-human animals, are all examples of distributed systems that exploit concurrency. In fact, the *genetic algorithm* which is the foundation for adaptation and natural selection is itself intrinsically parallel [Holland 1975]. The success of these mechanisms is sufficient grounds to interest one in the study of the implications of concurrent processing.

Overview

The rest of this chapter gives an overview of the book. The next chapter reviews the general design decisions that must be made in any model of concurrent computation. In Chapter 3 we describe the behavior of an actor and define a simple actor language which is used to show some specific examples of actors. In the following chapter, we define several higher level constructs which make the actor language more expressive and provide a mechanism for abstraction in actor systems. These constructs are definable in terms of the primitive actor constructs and are not considered as part of the *actor formalism*. The chapter defines an expressional language, and discusses different strategies for the evaluation of expressions.

Chapter 5 defines an *operational semantics* for actors by specifying a transition relation on configurations of actor systems. The guarantee of mail delivery is formalized by defining a second transition system which expresses this property. We take the primitive constructs of an actor language and show how one can provide an operational definition for them.

In Chapter 6, we are concerned with issues raised in related models. There are some significant difficulties in exploiting concurrency: distributed systems often exhibit pathological behavior such as divergence and deadlock. The actor model addresses these problems at a variety of levels. Divergence can be a useful property because of the guarantee of delivery;

deadlock in a strict sense does not exist in an actor system. Besides, the asynchronous, buffered nature of communication in actors provides mechanisms to detect deadlock in a semantic sense of the term. Chapter 6 also explores the relation between some aspects of dataflow and actors; in particular, the similarity between replacement in actors and what has been claimed to be the "side-effect free" nature of computation in both systems.

Chapter 7 tackles the issue of abstraction in actor systems. In particular, we discuss the nature of *open systems* and relate it to the insufficiency of the *history relation* observed in [Brock and Ackerman 1981]. The right level of abstraction would permit us to treat equivalent systems as semantically identical and yet differentiate systems between which an external observer can distinguish. We discuss the nature of composition in actors and show how we can model composition based on message-passing.

The final chapter summarizes some of the implications of the work in this book. Appendix A uses tools from Milner's work to define an abstract representation for actor systems in terms of what we call *Asynchronous Communication Trees*. This representation provides a suitable way of visualizing computations in actors.

Contributions

The specific contributions of this book are summarized below. This book provides:

- A critical overview of the characteristics of the various proposed models of concurrency.

- A simple outline of the actor model and the specification of minimal primitive constructs for actor languages.

- A transition system for actor systems and a structured operational semantics for an actor language.

- A paradigm for addressing problems in distributed computing that is suitable for computation in open systems.

- A model to support compositionality and abstraction from irrelevant detail.

Chapter 2

General Design Decisions

Several radically different programming languages for concurrent computation have been proposed. In this chapter, we will review the metalinguistic concepts in the model underlying each of the proposed programming languages. Our interest is in comparing and contrasting their primitives with a view towards determining their generality and applicability. Of particular concern to us is the relative ease with which massively concurrent architectures can be exploited. We will not describe different programming languages, or the models of computation underlying them, but will simply discuss the design decisions that characterize a system carrying out concurrent computation. The fundamental design decisions include:

- the nature of the computing elements

- global synchrony versus asynchronous elements

- the mode of interaction between computing elements

- the degree of fairness

- reconfigurability and extensibility

This list is by no means exhaustive but represents the aspects of a model of concurrent computation that we think are the most significant. There are other issues, such as the linguistic issues in the specification of a language based on any given model, but we will ignore these in our present discussion. We discuss each of the design issues in the sections that follow.

2.1   The Nature of Computing Elements

The elements performing computations are, in an abstract *denotational* sense, some kind of function. However, the domain and range of the functions defining the behavior of the elements is quite different in each of the models. Ignoring some significant details, we identify three distinct kinds of computational elements:

1. Sequential Processes.

2. Functions transforming data values.

3. Actors.

2.1.1   Sequential Processes

Sequential processes are inspired by algol-like procedures in sequential programming. Examples of systems based on the concept of sequential processes include *Concurrent Pascal* [Brinch Hansen 1977], *Communicating Sequential Processes* [Hoare 1978], and the *Shared Variables* model [Lynch and Fischer 1981]. Sequential processes are sequential in nature but can execute in parallel with each other.

The *operational* notion of a *sequential process* is that it performs a sequence of transformations on *states*, where a state is a map from *locations* to *values* such as integers. In addition, the transformations may depend on certain "inputs" to it and may produce certain "outputs," possibly in response to the inputs. It is this latter aspect which makes the denotational semantics of systems of sequential processes more difficult; in particular, explicit consideration of the possibility of deadlock (when a process is waiting for input that never arrives) is required [Brookes 1983].

2.1.2   Functions Transforming Data Values

A second kind of computational element is a *function* which acts directly on data without the benefit, or burden, of a store. Functional models are derived from λ-calculus based languages such as Pure Lisp [McCarthy 1959]. Examples of concurrent systems using some variant of the functional model include *dataflow* [Agerwala and Arvind 1982] and *networks of parallel processes* [Kahn and MacQueen 1978]. In dataflow architectures, *streams* of (data) values pass through functional agents [Weng 1975]. The concurrency in the system is a result of the ability to evaluate arguments of a function in parallel.

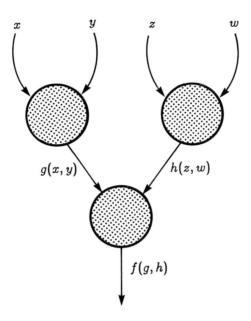

Figure 2.1: *An indeterminate applicative program. The arguments of functions are evaluated concurrently and the results fan in.*

Perhaps the simplest model of systems using functions is an *indeterminate applicative system* where call-by-value is used to evaluate the arguments and the result of the computation is a single value. Computation in such systems *fans in* as arguments are evaluated and passed along. Fig. 2.1 shows an example of concurrent evaluation in an *indeterminate applicative system.*

The functional elements may take several parameters as inputs but, given the parameters, can output only a single value. The same value may, however, be sent to different computational elements. Unfortunately, functions are *history insensitive* [Backus 1978]. This can be a problem when modeling the behavior of systems that can change their behavior over time. For example, consider the behavior of a *turnstile* with a counter which records the number of people passing through it. Each time the turnstile is turned, it reports a new number on the counter. Thus its behavior is not simply a function of a "turn" message but is sensitive to the prior history of the computation. The *turnstile* problem is essentially

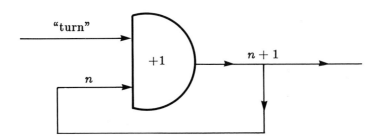

Figure 2.2: *History sensitive behavior can be implemented as a function with several arguments one of which is the value of the previous evaluation of the function itself.*

equivalent to that of generating the list of all positive integers, producing them one at a time in response to each message received.

In some 'functional' systems, the problem of history sensitive behavior is solved using feedback (i.e., by cyclic structures), as shown in Fig. 2.2 adapted from [Henderson 1980]. The turnstile is represented as a function of two inputs, a "turn" message and an integer n; in response to these inputs, the function produces the integer $n + 1$. The links act as *(first-in first-out) channels*, buffering the next value transmitted to the function, until the function of the previously transmitted arguments has been evaluated and it is ready to accept more input. (The same value is sent down all the links at a fork in the diagram.)

2.1.3   Actors

Actors are computational agents which map each incoming communication to a 3-tuple consisting of:

1. a finite set of communications sent to other actors;

2. a new behavior (which will govern the response to the next communication processed); and,

3. a finite set of new actors created.

Several observations are in order here. First, the behavior of an actor can be *history sensitive*. Second, there is *no presumed sequentiality* in the actions an actor performs: mathematically each of its actions is a function of the actor's behavior and the incoming communication. And finally, *actor creation* is an integral part of the computational model. An early precursor to the development of actors is the concept of objects in SIMULA [Dahl, Myhrhaug and Nygaard 1970] which represents containment in a single entity of data together with the operations and procedures on such data.

Actors are a more powerful computational agent than sequential processes or value-transforming functional systems. In other words, it is possible to define a purely functional system as an actor system, and it is possible to specify arbitrary sequential processes by a suitable actor system, but it is not possible to represent an arbitrary actor system as a system of sequential processes or as a system of value-transforming functions. To see how actors can be used to represent sequential processes or functional programs is not difficult: both are special cases of the more general actor model. If the reader is not convinced of this, the machinery developed later in this book should make it clear.

It is easy to see why the converse is true: actors may create other actors; value-transforming functions, such as the ones used in dataflow, can not create other functions; and sequential processes, as in *Communicating Sequential Processes*, do not create other sequential processes.[1] In the sequential paradigm of computation, the ability to create actors would not be significantly different from the ability to activate processes because the same computation could be formally represented in a system without actor creation. But in the context of parallel systems, the degree to which a computation can be *distributed* over its lifetime is an important consideration. Creation of new actors provides the ability to abstractly increase the distributivity of the computation as it evolves.

2.2 Global Synchrony and Asynchrony

The concept of a unique global clock is not meaningful in the context of a distributed system of self-contained parallel agents. This intuition was first axiomatized in [Hewitt and Baker 1977a] and was shown to be consistent with other *laws of parallel processing* in [Clinger 1981]. The reasoning here is analogous to that in special relativity: information in each computational agent is localized within that agent and must be communicated before it

---

[1] Sequential processes may activate other sequential processes and multiple activations are permitted but the topology of the individual process is still static. The difference between activation and creation is significant in the extent of reconfigurability afforded by each.

is known to any other agent. As long as one assumes that there are limits as to how fast information may travel from one computational agent to another, the local states of one agent as recorded by another agent relative to the second agent's local states will be different from observations done the other way round.

We may conclude that, for a distributed system, a *unique (linear) global time* is not definable. Instead, each computational agent has a local time which linearly orders the events as they occur at that agent, or alternately, orders the local states of that agent. These local orderings of events are related to each other by the *activation ordering*. The activation ordering represents the causal relationships between events happening at different agents. Thus the global ordering of events is a partial order in which events occurring at different computational agents are unordered unless they are connected, directly or indirectly, because of one or more causal links.

The lack of a unique global clock does not imply that it is impossible to construct a distributed system whose behavior is such that the elements of the system can be abstractly construed to be acting synchronously. An example of such a system is Cook's *hardware modification machine*. The hardware modification machine is a mathematical abstraction useful for studying the problems of computational complexity in the context of parallelism.

The problem of constructing a synchronously functioning system is essentially one of defining protocols to cope with a fundamental epistemological limitation in a distributed system. To see how the elements of a system can be construed to be *synchronous*, consider the example shown in Fig. 2.3.

Assume one element, called the *global synchronizer*, controls when each of the elements in the system may continue processing; all elements perform some predetermined number of actions, report to the global synchronizer and wait for another "go" message from the global synchronizer before proceeding. The global synchronizer knows how many elements there are in the system and waits for each of them to report before sending out the next "go" message. Conceptually, we can think of each of the elements acting synchronously and the system passing through execution cycles on a "global clock". We can ignore the precise *arrival order* of messages to the global synchronizer, because in such a system the exact order may be irrelevant.

The important point to be made is that any such global synchronization creates a bottleneck which can be extremely inefficient in the context of a distributed environment. Every process must wait for the slowest process to complete its cycle, regardless of whether there is any logical dependence of a process on the results of another. Furthermore, it is not altogether

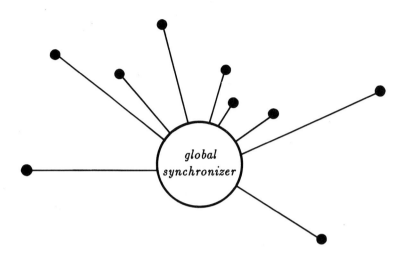

Figure 2.3: *A synchronizing mechanism: A global synchronizer controls the cycles of computation by each of the elements in the system. Each element carries out one step at a time and communicates with the global synchronizer for permission to carry out the next step.*

obvious that such global synchrony makes it any easier to write programs in general. Although systems designed to act synchronously may be useful in some particular applications, we will deal with the general asynchronous distributed environment; the behavior of the synchronous system can always be derived as a special case. (See, for example, the discussion in Chapter 4 of mechanisms involving an effectively prioritized exchange of communications between two actors.)

2.3   Interaction Between Agents

How the elements of a concurrent system affect each other is one of the most salient features of any model of concurrent computation. The proposed *modes of interaction* between the computational elements of a system can be divided into two different classes:

1. variables common to different agents; and,

2. communication between independent agents.

We take up these two modes of interaction in turn.

2.3.1 Shared Variables

The basic idea behind the *shared variables* approach is that the various processes can read and write to locations common to more than one process. When one process reads the contents of a location which has been changed by another, the subsequent behavior of the first process may be affected. This sort of common variables approach is taken in [Lynch and Fischer 1981].

The shared variables approach does <u>not</u> provide any mechanism for abstraction and information hiding. For instance, there must be predetermined protocols so that one process can determine if another has written the results it needs into the relevant variables. Similarly no mechanism is provided for protecting data against arbitrary and improper operations. One kind of paradigm of software engineering is to combine the procedural and declarative information into well-defined *objects* so that access to data is controlled and modularity is promoted in the system. This sort of *absolute containment* of information is also an important tool for *synchronizing* access to scarce resources and proving freedom from *deadlock*. Because the shared variables model fixes the level of atomicity of the actions (see the discussion about receptionists in Section 7.1.2), the programmer has the burden of specifying the relevant details to achieve meaningful interaction.

Another fundamental problem in using the shared variables approach in large-scale concurrent systems is that in order to read and write to common locations, the processes sharing a variable must be close to the location at which the value of the variable is stored. Otherwise, the *latency* in accessing the shared location would become a bottleneck. Communication for sharing information allows a greater degree of independence of the processes from each other.

2.3.2 Communication

Several models of concurrent computation use communication between independent computational agents. Communication provides a mechanism by which each agent retains the integrity of information within it. There are two possible assumptions about the nature of communication between independent computational elements; communication can be considered to be either:

- *synchronous*, where both the *sender* and the *receiver* of a communication must be ready to communicate before a communication can be sent; or,

- *asynchronous*, where the *receiver* does not have to be ready to accept a communication when the *sender* sends it.

Hoare's Communicating Sequential Processes and Milner's *Calculus of Communicating Systems* assume synchronous communication while the *actor model* [Hewitt and Baker 1977b] and *dataflow* [Ackerman 1984] do not. The telephone system is considered an example of a real-world system which uses synchronous communication (although since the advent of the answering machine this is no longer universally the case). The postal system is an example of a system which uses asynchronous communication.

We examine each assumption and its implications below. A concurrent computational environment is meaningful only in the context of a conceptually distributed system. Intuitively, there can be no action at a distance. This implies that before a sender can know that the receiver is "free" to accept a communication, it must send a communication to the receiver, and *vice-versa*. Thus one may conclude that any model of synchronous communication is built on asynchronous communication.

However, the fact that synchronous communication must be defined in terms of asynchronous communication does not necessarily imply that asynchronous communication is itself the right level of abstraction for programming. In particular, an argument could be made that synchronous communication should be provided in any programming language for concurrent computation if it provides a means of writing programs without being concerned with the detail which may be required in all computation. The question then becomes if synchronous communication is helpful as a universal assumption for a programming language. We examine this issue below.

2.3.3 The Need for Buffering

In this section, we show that synchronous communication is a special case of buffered asynchronous communication. In any system, every communication is of some finite length and takes some finite time to transmit. During the time that one communication is being sent, some computational agent may try to send another communication to the agent receiving the first communication. Certainly one would not want to interleave arbitrary bits of one communication with those of another! In some sense, we wish to preserve the *atomicity* of the communications sent. A solution to this problem is to provide a "secretary" to each agent which in effect tells all other agents attempting to communicate that the given agent is "busy." [2]

---

[2] This could be done for instance by simply not responding to an incoming communication.

Essentially, the underlying system could provide such a "secretary" in an implementation of a model assuming synchronous communication, as in a telephone network.

There is another problem in assuming synchronous communication. Suppose the sender is transmitting information faster than the receiver can accept it. For example, as this book is typed in on a terminal, the speed of the typist may at times exceed the rate at which the computer is accepting the characters. To get around this problem, one could require that the typist type only as fast as the *editing process* can accept the characters. This solution is obviously untenable as it amounts to typing one character at a time and waiting for a response (in fact, the argument would continue to the level of electrons!). The other solution is to provide the system with the capability to buffer the segments of a communication.

Of course, if the underlying system is required to buffer segments of a communication, it can equally well be required to buffer different communications so that the sender does not *have* to be "busy waiting" for the receiver to accept a communication before it proceeds to do some other processing. Thus *buffered asynchronous communication* affords us efficiency in execution by not arbitrarily delaying a computation which does not need to wait for another process to receive a given communication. Furthermore, synchronous communication can be defined in the framework of asynchronous communication.[3] The mechanism for doing so is simply "suspending" the sender until the receiver acknowledges the receipt of a communication [Hewitt and Atkinson 1977].

There is yet another significant advantage in buffered asynchronous communication. It may be important for a computational element to communicate with itself; in particular, this is the case when an element defines a recursive computation. However, communication with oneself is impossible if the *receiver* must be free when the *sender* sends a communication: because the *sender* will be "busy waiting" forever for itself to be free, this situation immediately leads to a *deadlock*. The problem actually is worse: no mutually recursive control structure is possible because of the same reason. Mutual recursion, however, may not be apparent simply by looking at the code. There is no *a priori* problem with such recursive structures if communications are buffered.

Both the *dataflow architecture* [Ackerman 1984] and the *Apiary architecture* for actor systems [Hewitt 1980] provide the capability to buffer

---

[3]The notion of synchrony as simultaneity is physically unrealizable. The *failure of simultaneity at a distance* occurs because whether two clocks are synchronous is itself dependent on the particular *frame of reference* in which the observations are carried out [Feynman, Leighton and Sands 1965]. We assume that any notion of synchronous communication is a conceptual one.

communications from asynchronous computing elements. However, it is not altogether obvious how the computational elements to provide for buffering communications can be defined in a functional language (as opposed to simply assumed). Thus it is not possible to produce a meta-circular definition of a dataflow language. In contrast, such buffers are readily defined in actor languages.

2.4 Nondeterminism and Fairness

Nondeterminism arises quite inevitably in a distributed environment. A cooperative paradigm of computation is meaningful only in the context of a distributed environment. In any real *network of computational agents*, one cannot predict precisely when a communication sent by one agent will arrive at another. This is particularly true when the network is *dynamic* and the underlying architecture is free to improve performance by *reconfiguring* the virtual computational elements. Therefore a realistic model must assume that the *arrival order* of communications sent is both arbitrary and entirely unknown. In particular, communications from different agents to a given target (and, in some cases, from the same agent), may arrive at approximately the same time. When this happens, it is necessary to provide a mechanism which orders incoming messages. This is achieved at the hardware level by an element called the *arbiter*. The use of the arbiter for serialization implies that the arrival order is physically indeterminate.

2.4.1 The Guarantee of Delivery

Given that a communication may be delayed for an arbitrarily long period of time, the question arises whether it is reasonable to assume that a communication sent is always delivered. In a purely physical context, the finiteness of the universe suggests that a communication sent ought to be delivered. On the other hand, the issue is whether buffering means that the *guarantee of delivery* of communications is impossible. There are, realistically, no *unbounded buffers* in the physically realizable universe. This is similar to the fact that there are no *unbounded stacks* in the universe, and certainly not in our processors, and yet we parse recursive control structures in algolic languages as though there were an infinite stack. The alternative to assuming unbounded space is that we have to assume some specific finite limit; but each finite limit leads to a different behavior. However, there is no general limit on buffers: the size of a real buffer will be specific to the constraints of a particular implementation. The point of building a semantic model is to abstract away from such details.

The guarantee of delivery of communications is, by and large, a property of well-engineered systems that should be modelled because it has significant consequences. If a system did not eventually deliver a communication it was buffering, it would have to buffer the communication indefinitely. The cost of such storage is obviously undesirable. The guarantee of delivery does not assume that every communication is "meaningfully" processed. For example, in the actor model the processing of communications is dependent on the behavior of individual actors, and there may be classes of actors which ignore all communications or indefinitely buffer some communications; buffering done internally by an actor is distinct from buffering done by the mail system. In the latter case, a communication cannot be buffered indefinitely.

The guarantee of mail delivery provides one with mechanisms to reason about concurrent programs so that results analogous to those established by reasoning about total correctness in sequential programs can be derived; in some cases, the guarantee helps prove termination properties.

2.4.2   Fairness and the Mail System

Not all algorithms for delivering communications result in a *mail system* that guarantees delivery. For instance, a mail system that always delivered the "shortest" communication in its buffer may not deliver every communication. Consider an actor in such a system which sends itself a "short" communication in response to a "short" communication. If a "long" and a "short" communication are concurrently sent to this actor, it is possible that the actor may never receive the "long" communication.

The guarantee of delivery is one form of what is called *fairness*. There are other forms of fairness, such as *fairness over arbitrary predicates*, or *extreme fairness* [Pnueli 1983] where probabilistic considerations are used. The guarantee of delivery of communications is perhaps the weakest form of fairness one can assume (although it is not clear what sort of formal framework one would define to establish this rigorously). The question arises as to whether one should assume a stronger form of fairness; for example, that the communications sent are received in a probabilistically random order regardless of any property they have.

Consider a system that chooses to deliver up to three "short" communications for every "long" communication it delivers (if the shorter communications are found). Such a system would still satisfy the requirement of guaranteeing delivery of communications, but would not satisfy some stronger fairness requirements, for example, the requirement that all communications sent have an equal probability of being the next to be delivered. At the same time, it may be very reasonable to have such an underlying *mail system* for some applications. We prefer to accept the guarantee of delivery of communications but not any form of fairness stronger than this guarantee. We will study the implications and usefulness of the guarantee later in this book.

Of course, given the lack of a unique order of events in a distributed system, what the definitions of stronger forms of fairness really mean is not altogether obvious. Our initial cognizance in such cases can sometimes be misleading because our intuitions are better developed for sequential processes whose behavior is qualitatively different. In particular, the mail system is itself distributed and, even according to a specific given observer, the delivery of communications to different agents may overlap in time.

2.5 Reconfigurability and Extensibility

The patterns of communication possible in any system of processes define a topology on those processes. Each process (or computational agent) may, at any given point in its local time, communicate with some set of processes. As the computation proceeds, a process may either communicate only with those processes that it could communicate with at the beginning of the computation, or it may evolve to communicate with other processes that it could not communicate with before. In the former case, the *interconnection topology* is said to be *static*; and in the latter, it is *dynamic*.

Any system of processes is somewhat easier to analyze if its interconnection topology is static: the graph representing the connections between the processes is constant and hence relatively more information about the system is available at compile time. Perhaps because of this structural simplicity in the analysis of static topologies, many models of concurrency assume that a process over its lifetime can communicate with only those very same processes that it could communicate with when it was first created. However, a static topology has severe limitations in representing the behavior of real systems. We illustrate these limitations by means of the following example.

2.5.1 A Resource Manager

Consider the case of a *resource manager* for two printing devices. We may assume for our present purposes that the two devices are identical in their behavior and therefore interchangeable. One would like this resource manager to:

1. Send *print requests* to the first available printing device.

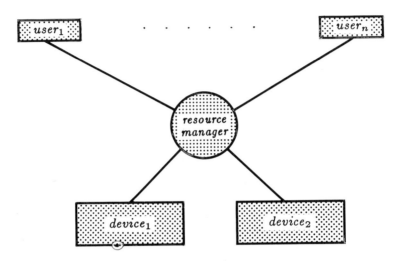

Figure 2.4: *A static graph linking the* resource manager *to two devices and two users. Such graphs are an unsatisfactory representation of systems that may dynamically evolve to include new users or devices.*

2. Once a *print request* has been processed, send a *receipt* to the user requesting the printing.

These requirements imply that the resource manager be able to communicate with a different device each time. Thus a system in which the communication links were static and communications were sent down these links, without the resource manager being able to choose which link ought to be used, would either send a communication to both the devices or to neither. This is the situation in a dataflow graph shown in Fig. 2.4. However, the resource manager should be able to choose where it wants to send a communication (depending on which device is free), suggesting that the *edges* of the graph represent only potential communication channels and not actual ones. The true links would be determined dynamically.[4]

---

[4]It is possible to define a more complex dataflow graph using specific nodes called *switches* which permit dynamic routing of tokens. Different dataflow models add different special elements to cope with such practical problems. However, such elements are often semantic extensions to the model since they cannot be defined in terms of other dataflow constructs.

Requiring that a receipt be sent to the user introduces other complications. For one, the number of users may vary with time. This variation by itself creates the need for a dynamic graph on the processes [Brock 1983]. For another, the maximum number of users need not be constant. In a system that might evolve to include more resources, the addition of the increased capacity should be graceful and not require the redefinition of the entire system. This implies that a solution using a fixed number of *communication channels* is not very satisfactory in an *open system* which is constantly subject to growth. (For a discussion of open systems see [Hewitt and deJong 1983]). For instance, if we wanted to add a third printing device, we should not necessarily have to program another resource manager, but rather should be able to define a resource manager which can incorporate the presence of a new printing device when sent an appropriate message to that effect.

A system that is not only *reconfigurable* but *extensible* is powerful enough to handle these problems. Because the ability to gracefully extend a system is dependent on the ability to relate the extension to the elements of the system that are already in existence, reconfigurability is the logical pre-requisite for extensibility of a system. An elegant solution to the problem of resource management using an actor system can be found in [Hewitt, et al 1985].

2.5.2　The Dynamic Allocation of Resources

Extensibility has other important consequences. It allows a system to dynamically allocate resources to a problem by generating computational agents in response to the magnitude of a computation required to solve a problem. The precise magnitude of the problem need not be known in advance: more agents can be created as the computation proceeds and the maximal amount of concurrency can be exploited.

For example, consider a "balanced addition" problem, where the addition has to be performed on a set of real numbers. If the numbers are added sequentially,

$$(...(((a_1 + a_2) + a_3) + a_4) + ... + a_n)$$

then there is a classic problem of "propagation of errors," discussed in [vonNeumann 1958]. The problem occurs because real numbers are implemented using floating-point registers. Computational errors, instead of being statistically averaged, become *fixed* as rounding errors move to more significant bits. It is preferable to add the numbers in pairs,

$$(...(((a_1 + a_2) + (a_3 + a_4)) + ((a_5 + a_6) + (...))) + ... + (a_{n-1} + a_n)...)$$

which results in the error being statistically reduced by the "law of large numbers."

Addition in pairs is well suited to concurrent computation because it can be done using parallel computation in log-time, as opposed to linear time when carried out sequentially. Now if we had a program to carry out this addition in pairs, we may want the program to work even if we input a different number of real numbers each time. Thus we can <u>not</u> define a static network to deal with this problem [vanEmden and Filho 1982]. Addition in pairs is easily accomplished in an actor system by creating other actors, called *customers* (see Example 3.2.2), which have the behavior of adding two numbers sent to them in two consecutive communications. The evaluations are carried out concurrently and the replies sent to the appropriate customers. Such concurrency is the default in actor languages.

Reconfigurability in actor systems is obtained using the *mail system* abstraction. Each actor has a *mail address* which may be freely communicated to other actors, thus changing the interconnection network of the system of actors as it evolves. We develop a specific model for actor systems in the chapters that follow.

Chapter 3

Computation In Actor Systems

In this chapter, we examine the structure of computation in the actor paradigm. The discussion here will be informal and intuitive, deferring consideration of the technical aspects to later chapters. The organization of this chapter is as follows. In the first section, we explain actors and communications. In the second section, we outline the constructs which suffice to define a minimal actor language. We give some examples of actor programs to illustrate the constructs using structured "pseudo-code." In the final section, kernels of two simple actor languages are defined and a program example is expressed in each of these languages. The two languages, SAL and *Act*, are minimal but sufficient for defining all possible actor systems. SAL follows an algol-like syntax while *Act* uses a Lisp-like syntax. In the next chapter, we will define some new linguistic constructs, but these constructs will not be foundational; they can be defined using a minimal actor language. These extensions to a minimal language illustrate the power of the primitive actor constructs.

3.1 Defining an Actor System

Computation in a system of actors is carried out in response to communications sent to the system. Communications are contained in *tasks*. As computation proceeds, an actor system evolves to include new tasks and new actors that are created as a result of processing tasks already in the system. All tasks that have already been processed and all actors that are no longer "useful," may be removed (in other words, *garbage collected*) from the system without affecting its subsequent behavior.[1] The *configuration* of an *actor system* is defined by the actors it contains as well as the set of unprocessed tasks.

3.1.1   Tasks

In somewhat simplified terms, we can say that the unprocessed tasks in a system of actors are the driving force behind computation in the system. We represent a *task* as a 3-tuple consisting of:

1. a *tag* which distinguishes it from all other tasks in the system;

2. a *target* which is the mail address to which the communication is to be delivered; and,

3. a *communication* which contains information made available to the actor at the target, when that actor processes the given task.

As a simplification, we will consider a communication to be a tuple of values. The values may be mail addresses of actors, integers, strings, or whatever, and we may impose a suitable type discipline on such values. There are other possible models here; perhaps the most exciting of these models, and the one using the greatest uniformity of construction, is one in which the communications are themselves actors.[2] In such a model, communications may themselves be sent communications. For example, if we want a communication k_1 to print itself, we could send a communication k_2 to the communication k_1 which asked k_1 to print itself. The semantic theory of actors is, however, considerably complicated by modelling communications as actors, and we therefore do not do so.[3]

Before an actor can send an another actor a communication, it must know the *target* actor's mail address [Hewitt and Baker 1977a]. There are three ways in which an actor α, upon accepting a communication $\bar{k}$, can know of a target to which it can send a communication. These are:

- the target was known to the actor α before it accepted the communication $\bar{k}$,

---

[1] We refer here to the semantic equivalence of the systems with and without "garbage." Of course, the performance of the system is a different matter.

[2] The behavior of an actor is to send communications to other actors it knows about (i.e., its *acquaintances*), which in turn do the same until the communications are received by pre-defined *built-in actors* such as numbers and primitive pre-defined operations (See Section 4.4.). In the more general *universe of actors model*, tasks themselves are actors which have three *acquaintances*, namely the three components of the tuple given above.

[3] For a discussion of the *universe of actors* model see Section 4.4.

- the target became known when α accepted the communication $\bar{k}$ which contained the target, or

- the target is the mail address of a new actor created as a result of accepting the communication $\bar{k}$.

A *tag* helps us to uniquely identify each task by distinguishing between tasks which may contain identical targets and communications. We will make use of the uniqueness of each tag when we define an operational semantics for actor systems. An important observation that should be made here is that any particular representation of the tags is somewhat arbitrary. Tags are used because they are useful in distinguishing between tasks. However, the tasks themselves are existentially distinct entities.

There are various ways of representing tags; one such representation is a string of nonnegative integers separated by "." (periods). Using this representation, if ω is a tag for task t, then $\omega.n$, where n is some nonnegative integer, can be the tag for some task created as a result of processing t. In this way, if we start with a set of tags uniquely associated with the tasks, we can guarantee that all tasks always have distinct tags (by using a restriction that the last number appended is distinct for each task created by the same actor in response to the same communication). Note that there may be only a <u>finite</u> number of tasks in any given system.

3.1.2 The Behavior of an Actor

As we discussed earlier, all computation in an actor system is the result of processing communications. This is somewhat similar to a *data-driven* system like dataflow, and in contrast to systems based on processes that either terminate or are perpetually "active." Actors are said to *accept* a communication when they process a task containing that communication. An actor may process only those tasks whose target corresponds to its mail address. When an actor accepts a communication, it may create new actors or tasks; it must also compute a replacement behavior.

For any given actor, the *order of arrival* of communications sent to that actor is a linear order. In particular, this implies that the *mail system* must provide suitable mechanisms for *buffering* and *arbitration* of incoming communications when such communications arrive at roughly the same time. The mail system places the communications sent to a given target on the *mail queue* corresponding to that target. For most purposes, it is appropriate to consider the mail queue as part of the mail system. However, when we wish to deal with issues related to the *arrival order* of communications,

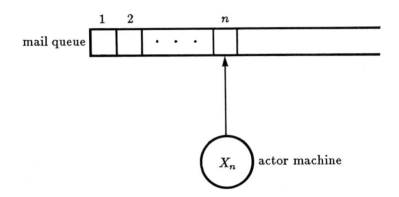

Figure 3.1: *An abstract representation of an actor. The actor machine contains information that determines the behavior of an actor. It accepts the current communication and cannot access information from any other communication.*

such as the *guarantee of mail delivery*,[4] we have to consider the mail queue explicitly.

An actor may be described by specifying:

- its mail address, to which there corresponds a sufficiently large *mail queue*[5]; and,

- its *behavior*, which is a function of the communication accepted.

Abstractly, we may picture an actor with a mail queue on which all communications are placed in the order in which they arrive and an *actor machine*[6] which points to a particular cell in the mail queue. The end of a

---

[4] The presence of communication failures in a real system should not be considered a hindrance for a theoretical investigation assuming a reliable mail system. See the related discussion in Section 2.4.

[5] The mail queue will be considered large enough to hold all communications sent to a given actor. This implies that a mail queue is, in principle, unbounded, while only a finite fragment of it is used at any given point in time. This is quite similar to a read-only tape of a Turing Machine. However, the writing is done indirectly using the mail system.

[6] No assumption should be made about an actor machine being sequential. Like machines in the real world, an actor machine may have components that function in parallel.

communication on the mail queue can be indicated by some special symbol reserved for the purpose.[7] We represent this pictorially as in Fig. 3.1.

When an actor machine X_n accepts the $n\underline{th}$ communication in a mail queue, it will create a new actor machine, X_{n+1}, which will carry out the replacement behavior of the actor. The new actor machine will point to the cell in the mail queue in which the $n + 1\underline{st}$ communication is (or will be) placed. This can be pictorially represented as in Fig. 3.2.

The two actor machines X_n and X_{n+1} will <u>not</u> affect each other's behavior: X_n processes only the $n\underline{th}$ communication. (Of course, if X_n sends a communication to the actor it represents the current state of, X_{n+1} may be the actor machine which processes that communication.) Specifically, each of the actor machines may create their own tasks and actors as defined by their respective behaviors. Before the machine X_n creates X_{n+1}, X_n may of course have already created some actors and tasks; however, it is also possible that X_n may still be in the process of creating some more tasks and actors even as X_{n+1} is doing the same. In any event, note that the machine X_n will neither receive any further communications nor specify any other replacement.[8]

If we define an *event* as the creation of a new task, then the order of events that are caused by the acceptance of a communication is a partial order. An event results in the creation of new tasks and actors and the specification of a replacement behavior. The replacement machines at any mail address have a total order between them. This linear order is isomorphic to the arrival order of the corresponding communications which result in their replacement (as may be readily inferred from Fig. 3.2).

An event-based picture for computation with actors uses *life-lines* which are shown in Fig. 3.3. Each actor has an order of acceptance of communications which is linear. The events in the life of an actor are recorded in the order in which they occur: the further down the line, the later in local time. Activations (causal ordering of events) are indicated by the lines connecting two different actors with the arrow on the line indicating causal direction. A lifeline may also be labeled by the pending communications, i.e., by communications that have been received but not processed. Clinger [Clinger 1981] used collections of lifelines augmented with pending communications to provide a fixed-point semantics for actors. The resulting pictures are called *actor event diagrams*.

A couple of general remarks about the implementation issues are in order here:

---

[7]Thus the variable length of a communication is not a problem.

[8]We will later model functions that require more input as a collection of these elemental actors.

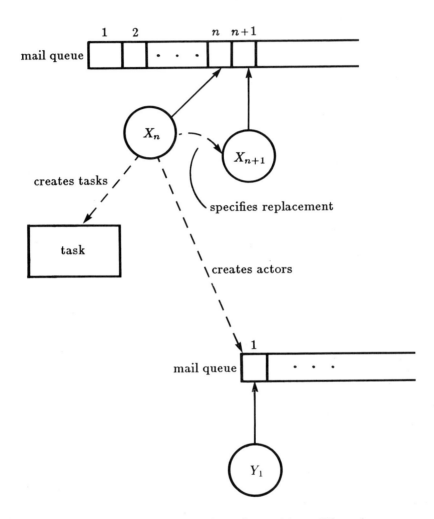

Figure 3.2: *An abstract representation of transition. When the actor processes the $n\underline{th}$ communication, it determines the replacement behavior which will process the $n + 1\underline{st}$ communication. The replacement behavior is encapsulated in a new actor machine. The mail address of the actor remains invariant. The actor may also send communications to specific target actors and create new actors.*

Remark 1. The reader may wonder about the efficiency of constructing a new actor machine in response to each communication accepted. It should be emphasized that this is simply a conceptual assumption that frees us from the details of any particular implementation. *Concurrency* simply means *potential* parallelism. Some implementations may find it useful to generally delay constructing the replacement until the old machine can be cannibalized. However, delaying the construction of the replacement is not a universal requirement as would be the case in a sequential machine. Thus, if there are sufficient resources available, computation in an actor system can be speeded up by an order of magnitude by simply proceeding with the next communication as soon as the ontological necessity of determining the replacement behavior has been satisfied. The advantages of this kind of *pipelining* can be illustrated by the following simple example: Consider a calculation which requires $\mathcal{O}(n^2)$ sequential steps to carry out, where $\mathcal{O}(n)$ represents the size of input. Suppose further that computing the replacements in this computation takes only $\mathcal{O}(n)$ steps. If we had a static architecture with $\mathcal{O}(m)$ processes, it would take $\mathcal{O}(n^2)$ cycles per calculation. By pipelining, an actor-based architecture could carry out m calculations in the same time as a single calculation because it would initiate the next computation as soon as the replacement for the previous one had been computed—a process taking only $\mathcal{O}(n)$ steps.

Remark 2. It should also be pointed out that the structure of an actor machine is extremely concurrent: when any particular segment of the computation required by the acceptance of a communication has been completed, the resources used by the corresponding fragment of the "machine" are immediately available. It may be difficult, if one thinks in terms of sequential processes, to conceive of the inherent parallelism in the actions of an actor. The structure of computation in a sequential process is linear: typically, activations of procedures are stacked, each activation storing its current state. However, in an actor program, the absence of *assignment commands* permits the concurrent execution of the commands in a specification of the behavior of an actor. We will discuss the specific mechanisms for spawning concurrency, such as the use of *customers* to continue computations required for a transaction, later in this chapter.

3.2 Programming With Actors

In this section, we define the constructs necessary for the *kernel* of a minimal actor language. We also give some simple examples of actor programs. These examples illustrate, among other things, the versatility of message-passing as a general mechanism for implementing control structures, pro-

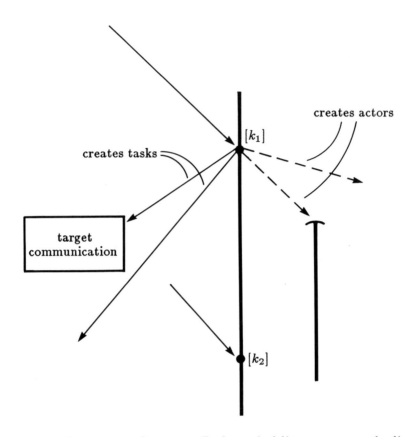

Figure 3.3: *Actor event diagrams. Each vertical line represents the linear arrival order of communications sent to an actor. In response to processing the communications, new actors are created and different actors may be sent communications which arrive at their target after an arbitrary delay.*

cedure and data abstraction in the concept of an actor, and the use of mail addresses instead of pointer types in data structures. The feasibility of representing control structures as patterns of message-passing was first described in [Hewitt 1977].

Despite its simplicity, the kernel of an actor language is extremely powerful: it captures several important features of computation in the actor paradigm; among them, the ability to distribute a computation between concurrent elements, the ability to spawn the maximal concurrency allowed by the control structure, the unification of procedural and declarative information, data abstraction and absolute containment.

An actor accepts a single communication as "input." Thus, if a computation is a function of communications from several different actors, it has to be defined using either a system of actors or an actor with the ability to buffer communications. We will introduce linguistic constructs to simplify expressing some multi-input functions in a transparent manner (see Section 4.1). All such constructs can be defined in terms of actors whose behavior is expressed in a minimal actor language. Without loss of generality, we confine our present discussion to the constructs necessary for a kernel language.

3.2.1 The Basic Constructs

To define the initial configuration of an actor system we need the ability to create some actors and send them communications. We promote modularity by specifying the actors which may communicate with the "outside," i.e., with actors not defined within the configuration. A program in an actor language consists of:

- *behavior definitions* which simply associate a behavior schema with an identifier (without actually creating an actor).[9]

- *new expressions* which create actors.

- *send commands* which create tasks.

- *a receptionist declaration* which lists actors that may receive communications from the outside.

- *an external declaration* which lists actors that are not part of the population defined by the program but to whom communications may be sent from within the configuration.

We discuss the syntax and intended meaning for each of the expressions which can be used in a minimal language. For some simple expressions, we also show what a feasible syntax might be.

---

[9]Such behavior schemas are not considered to be actors in the simple model we are currently using. In another language, such definitions can be used to create actors which are "descriptions" of actor behaviors. The behavior of such *description actors* would be to create actors of the given description when sent an appropriate communication.

Defining Behaviors

Each time an actor accepts a communication, it computes a replacement behavior. Since each replacement behavior will also have a replacement behavior, in order to specify the behavior of an actor we need to specify a potentially infinite definition. Obviously one cannot write an infinite string to define each replacement. Fortunately, we can use the *principle of recursive* (or *inductive*) *definition* so familiar from mathematics. Essentially, we parameterize each expressible behavior by some identifier which will be a free variable in the definition. Whenever a behavior is specified using the behavior definition, we must specify specific values for the identifiers parameterizing the behavior definition. For example, the behavior of a bank-account depends on the balance in the account. We therefore specify the behavior of every account as a function of the balance. Whenever a particular account is created, or a replacement behavior specified, which uses the behavior definition of a bank-account, a specific value for the balance in the account must be given.

There are also an infinite number of possible values for the incoming communication. Therefore, a behavior definition is expressed as a function of the incoming communication.

Two lists of identifiers are used in a behavior definition. Values for the first list of parameters must be specified when the actor is created. This list is called the *acquaintance list*. The second list of parameters, called the *communication list*, gets its bindings from an incoming communication. An actor executes commands in its script in the *environment* defined by the bindings of the identifiers in the acquaintance and communication lists.

Creating Actors

An actor is created using a *new expression* which returns the mail address of a newly created actor. The mail address returned should be bound to either an identifier or used directly in message-passing; otherwise, it would not have been useful to have created the actor. The syntax of new expressions would be something corresponding to the following:

$$\langle new\ expression \rangle ::= \ \textbf{new}\ \langle beh\ name \rangle\ (\ \{expr\ \{\ ,\ expr\ \}^* \}\ )$$

The ⟨*beh name*⟩ corresponds to an identifier bound to a behavior given by a declaration using a *behavior definition*. A new actor is created with the behavior implied by the *behavior definition* and its parameters, if any, are instantiated to the values of the expressions in the parentheses. In actor jargon, we have specified the *acquaintances* of an actor. The value of the expression is the mail address of the actor created and it can be bound by a

⟨*let command*⟩ to an identifier called an *actor name*. An *actor name* may be used as the target of any communication, including communications sent in the initial configuration.

Actors created concurrently by an actor may know each other's mail addresses.[10] This is a form of mutually recursive definition permissible in actors. However, all the newly created actor knows is the mail address of the other actor; it does not have any direct access to the internal structure of that actor.

Creating Tasks

A task is created by specifying a target and a communication. Communications may be sent to actors that already exist, or to actors that have been newly created by the sender. The target is the mail address of the actor to which the communication is sent. The syntax of a command that would create tasks is something like the one given below:

$$\langle send\ command \rangle ::= \quad \text{send } \langle communication \rangle \text{ to } \langle target \rangle$$

where a *communication* is a sequence of expressions (perhaps empty). The expressions may be identifiers, constants, or the appropriate functions of these. The expressions are evaluated and the corresponding values are sent in the communication. The *target* is an expression which evaluates to the mail address of an actor.

Declaring Receptionists

Although creating actors and tasks is sufficient to specify an actor system, simply doing so does not provide a mechanism for abstracting away the internal details of a system and concentrating on the behavior of the actor system as it would be viewed by its external environment. In order to reason about the composition of independently defined and debugged systems, and to permit greater modularity in a system, we allow the programmer to specify the initial set of *receptionists* for a system. The receptionists are the only actors that are free to receive communications from outside the system. Since actor systems are dynamically evolving and open in nature, the set of receptionists may also be constantly changing. Whenever a communication containing a mail address is sent to an actor outside the

---

[10]The possibility that concurrently created actors can know each other's mail address is simply for programming convenience. It is possible to create two actors sequentially and send the first actor the mail address of the second. To figure out the details of the mechanism, see the discussion of *insensitive actors* (used for locking) in Section 4.2 and of sequential composition in Section 4.3.

system, the actor residing at that mail address can receive communications from the outside and therefore *become* a receptionist. Thus the set of receptionists may increase as the system evolves.

If no receptionists are declared, the system cannot initially receive communications from actors outside the system. However, the mail address of an actor may subsequently be delivered to an external actor, so that the actor system may evolve to include some receptionists. This illustrates the potentially dynamic nature of the set of receptionists.

Declaring External Actors

Communications may be sent to actors outside an actor system. In a communication from the outside, an actor may get the mail address of another actor which is not in the system. It would then be able to send communications to the external actor. However, even when an actor system is being defined, it may be intended that it be a part of a larger system composed of independently developed modules. Therefore, we allow the ability to declare a sequence of identifiers as *external*. The compiler may associate these identifiers with actors whose behavior is to buffer the communications they accept. Whenever a given actor system is composed with another in which the external actors are actually specified, the buffered mail can be forwarded to the mail address of the actual actor which was hitherto unknown. External actors are thus implemented as *futures*—i.e., as actors whose intended identity is determined sometime after their creation. In Section 7.2 we show how concurrent composition using message-passing can be actually implemented in an open, evolving system.

There need be no external declaration in a program. In this case, initially no communication can be sent to mail addresses outside the actor system defined by the program. However, as the system receives communications from the outside, the set of external actors may "grow." Notice that it is useless to have an actor system which has neither receptionists nor external actors—such an autistic system will never affect the outside world!

Commands

The purpose of commands is to specify actions that are to be carried out. We have already discussed the basic commands which would create new actors and new tasks. We also need a command to specify a replacement behavior. The syntax of the *become command* in SAL is:

$$\text{become } \langle expression \rangle$$

where ⟨*expression*⟩ evaluates to a *behavior*. The actor may then process the next communication in its mail queue with the behavior specified (see Fig. 3.2).

One example of a behavior is that of a *forwarder*. A forwarder has one acquaintance, namely the actor to whom the communications must be forwarded. The acquaintance may be defined by a *new expression* in which case an actor is created with the given behavior and the forwarder forwards all communications to the newly created actor. If the acquaintance is an already existing actor then operationally the actor *becomes* a forwarding actor to the existing actor.

Sending a communication to an actor which is a *forwarder* is equivalent to sending the communication to the acquaintance of the *forwarder*. This abstract equivalence would not be valid in a model which did not assume arrival order nondeterminism and the guarantee of mail delivery. On the other hand, despite the message-passing equivalence of the two actors, they are not equal. Because the mail addresses of the two actors are distinct, subtle problems can arise if some code simply compares their mail addresses.

One other kind of command is necessary: a *conditional command* which causes one to branch to some segment of the code. Conditional or branching commands are of the usual *if-then* or *case* forms. It is also useful to allow *let bindings* so that identifiers may serve as a shorthand for expressions in a particular context. We have already seen the use of *let* bindings in the recording of the mail addresses of newly created actors.

Default Behaviors

Since all actors must specify a replacement behavior, we use the default that whenever there is no executable become command in the code of an actor in response to some communication, then we replace that actor with an identically behaving actor. Since the behavior of an actor is determined by a finite length script involving only conditional commands for control flow, it is can be thought of as a finite depth tree whose branches are executed. Because commands may be concurrent, it is possible that more than one branch will be executed. However, if we label the branches by the parameter representing the possible values of the communication, the tree is finite splitting. Thus only a finite number of actions may occur, and it is (easily) decidable if no replacement has been specified for a given acquaintance and communication list.

3.2.2 Examples

We define several examples of programs written using actors. These examples illustrate the relative ease with which various *data structures* and *control structures* can be implemented in an actor language. Specifically, we will give the implementation of a *stack* as a "linked list" of actors. This simple example also illustrates how the acquaintance structure makes the need for pointer types superfluous in an actor language. Other data structures can be defined in a similar manner.

The second example we present is that of the *recursive factorial function*. This is a classic example used in (almost) any work on actors. An iterative control structure can also be easily defined [Hewitt 1977]. The technique for an iterative factorial is similar to the standard *accumulation of parameters* in functional programming. We leave the details of the definition of an iterative factorial as an exercise for the interested reader. The final example in this section is an implementation of an actor specified by an external declaration. This example should clarify the use of external declarations to bind actors that are in the population of some independent module. The independent module can later be composed with the module presently being specified. We will deal with some more complex examples in the next chapter.

Example 3.2.1 A Stack. We implement a stack as a collection of actors with uniform behavior. As is always the case, these actors represent total containment of data as well as the operations valid on such data. Assume that the linked list consists of a collection of nodes each of which stores a value and knows the mail address of the "next" actor in the chain. The code for defining a stack element is given below. We skip the code for error handling because such details would simply detract from the basic behavior being expressed. We assume that there is a pre-defined value NIL and use it as a bottom of the stack marker. Two kinds of operations may be requested of a *stack-node*: a *push* or a *pop*. In the first case, the new content to be pushed must be given, and in the second, the customer to which the value stored in the *stack-node* can be sent.

> a *stack-node* with acquaintances *content* and *link*
>> if *operation requested is a pop* $\land$ *content* $\neq$ NIL **then**
>>> become *forwarder to link*
>>> send *content* to *customer*
>> if *operation requested is push* **then**
>>> let $P =$ **new** *stack-node with current acquaintances*
>>> { **become** *stack-node* with acquaintances *new-content and P* }

The top of the stack is the only receptionist in the stack system and was the only actor of the stack system created externally. It is created with a NIL content which is assumed to be the bottom of the stack marker. Notice that no mail address of a stack node is ever communicated by any node to an external actor. Therefore no actor outside the configuration defined above can affect any of the actors inside the stack except by sending the receptionist a communication. When a *pop* operation is done, the actor on top of the stack simply becomes a *forwarder* to the the next actor in the link. This means that all communications received by the top of the stack are now forwarded to the next element.

For those concerned about implementation efficiency, notice that the underlying architecture can splice through any chain of *forwarding actors* since forwarding actors have a static unserialized behavior and the configuration is unaffected by splicing through them. The forwarding actors can subsequently be garbage collected since they will not be the target of any tasks. The user is entirely free from considering the details of such optimizations.

Example 3.2.2 A Recursive Factorial. We give this classic example of a recursive control structure to illustrate the use of *customers* in implementing continuations. The example is adapted from [Hewitt 1977] which provided the original insight exploited here. In a sequential language, a recursive formula is implemented using a stack of activations. There is no mechanism in the sequential structure for distributing the work of computing a factorial or concurrently processing more than one request.

Our implementation of the *factorial actor* relies on creating a *customer* which waits for the appropriate communication, in this case from the factorial actor itself. The factorial actor is free to concurrently process the next communication. We assume that a communication to a factorial includes a mail address to which the value of the factorial is to be sent. The code for a recursive factorial is given below. Note that we use *self* as the mail address of the actor itself. This mail address will be instantiated when an actor is actually created using the *behavior definition* and serves as shorthand by eliminating the need for an extra parameter in the definition.

> *Rec-Factorial* with acquaintances *self*
> let *communication be an integer n and a customer u*
>> become *Rec-Factorial*
>> if $n = 0$
>> then send $[\,1\,]$ to *customer*
>> else let $c = Rec\text{-}Customer$ with acquaintances n *and* u
>>> {send $[n - 1$, *the mail address of c*] to *self* }

Rec-Customer with acquaintances *an integer n and a customer u*
  let *communication be an integer k*
     { send $[n * k]$ to u }

In response to a communication with a non-zero integer, n, the actor
with the above behavior will do the following:

- Create an actor whose behavior will be to multiply n with an integer it
  receives and send the reply to the mail address to which the factorial
  of n was to be sent.

- Send itself the "request" to evaluate the factorial of $n - 1$ and send
  the value to the customer it created.

One can intuitively see why the factorial actor behaves correctly, and
can use induction to prove that it does so. Provided the *customer* is sent the
correct value of the factorial of $n - 1$, the *customer* will correctly evaluate
the factorial of n. What's more, the evaluation of one factorial doesn't have
to be completed before the next request is processed; i.e., the factorial
actor can be a shared resource concurrently evaluating several requests.
The behavior of the factorial actor in response to a single initial request is
shown in Fig. 3.4.

This particular function is not very complicated, with the consequence
that the behavior of the *customer* is also quite simple. In general, the
behavior of the customer can be arbitrarily complex. The actor originally
receiving the request delegates most of the processing required by the request to a large number of actors, each of whom is dynamically created.
Furthermore, the number of such actors created is in direct proportion to
the magnitude of the computation required.

There is nothing inherently concurrent in the recursive algorithm to
evaluate a factorial. Using the above algorithm, computation of a single
factorial would <u>not</u> be any faster if it were done using an actor language as
opposed to a sequential language. All we have achieved is a representation
of the stack for recursion as a chain of customers. However, given a network
of processors, an actor-based language could process a large number of
requests much faster by simply distributing the actors it creates among
these processors. The factorial actor itself would not be as much of a
bottleneck for such computations.

In general more parallel algorithms for evaluating many common functions exist, and such algorithms can be exploited in an actor-based language. For example, a parallel method of evaluating a factorial treats
the problem as that of multiplying the range of numbers from 1...n. The
problem is recursively subdivided into multiplying two subranges. Such an

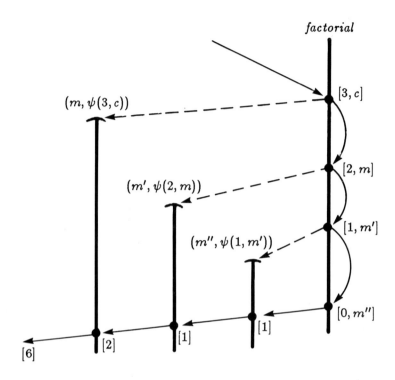

Figure 3.4: *A recursive factorial computation: the computation in response to a request to evaluate the factorial of 3. Each actor is denoted by a mail address and a behavior. The ψ's represent the behavior of the dynamically created customers. For example, the behavior $\psi(3, c)$ sends $[3 * k]$ to the mail address c in response to the communication k. (See text).*

algorithm results in the possibility of computing a single factorial in *log n* parallel time.

Example 3.2.3 External Actors. An actor program defines an initial configuration with its external actors defined by an ⟨*external declaration*⟩. To promote composition of independently programmed modules, the external actors are compiled in a specific manner. This example simply illustrates how one might implement external actors. The desired behavior of an external actor is to:

- simply hold all communications sent to it until the system is composed with another that contains the actor in question.

- respond to a communication telling it to forward all its mail to the actual actor when the composition is carried out.

In response to an external declaration, we actually create an actor which will exhibit the above behavior.

The code for an implementation can be given as follows. Assume that an actor called *buffer* is simultaneously created and, appropriately enough, buffers all communications until it accepts a communication telling it to forward them to a given mail address. Such a buffer could be specified as a queue using a linked list in a manner analogous to the implementation of the stack given above. One could also be a bit perverse and specify the buffer as a stack without changing the correctness of its behavior (recall the arrival order nondeterminism of the communications). As a stack, the behavior of the buffer would be given as below:

buffer with acquaintances *content and link*
    if *operation requested is release* $\land$ *content* $\neq$ NIL then
        send *content* to *customer*
        send *release request with customer* to *link*
        become *forwarder to customer*
    if *operation requested is hold* then
        let *B* be a new *buffer* with acquaintances *content and link*
        { become new *buffer* with acquaintances *new-content and B* }

Assume for the purposes of simplification that a protocol for specifying a communication to become a forwarding actor to the actor at the mail address m exists and that such a communication has the form become *forwarder to m*, where m is the mail address of the actor to which the mail should be forwarded. The behavior of an external actor, *extern*, is specified as below:

extern with acquaintances *buffer*
    if *the communication is become forwarder to customer*
      then become *forwarder to customer*
           send *release request with customer* to *buffer*
      else send *hold request with customer* to *buffer*

3.3   Minimal Actor Languages

In this section, we give the syntax for two minimal languages, SAL and *Act*. The programming language SAL has been developed for pedagogical reasons and follows an algol-like syntax. *Act* is related to the languages implemented by the Message Passing Semantics Group at M.I.T. and follows a lisp-like syntax. *Act* can be considered as a kernel for the *Act3* language [Hewitt, et al 1985]. One basic difference between SAL and *Act* is in how they bind identifiers and provide for their authentication. SAL uses conventional *type-checking* whereas *Act* uses an elaborate *description system* based on a lattice structure for reasoning with the descriptions. Because is·ues related to type-checking are not germane to our discussion, we omit types or descriptions from our syntax. The rest of this book will use expressions whose syntax was given in the previous section. For simple examples we will use SAL's syntax. However, it is not necessary to look at the details of the syntax in this section: the only feature of SAL's syntax that the reader needs to know is that the acquaintance list is enclosed in (...) while the communication list is enclosed in [...].

Notation. The usual Backus-Naur form is used. In particular, ⟨...⟩ encloses nonterminal symbols. We use darker letters for the terminals and *id* for identifiers. {...} is used to enclose optional strings, and a superscripted ∗ indicates 0 or more repetitions of the string are permissible, while a superscripted + indicates 1 or more repetitions of the string is permissible. When a reserved symbol, such as {, is underlined, it stands for itself and not for its usual interpretation.

3.3.1 A Simple Actor Language

We give the syntax for the kernel of SAL. Behavior definitions in a SAL program are *declarative* in the same sense as procedure declarations in an algol-like language: behavior definitions do <u>not</u> create any actors but simply bind an identifier to a behavior template. Actors are created by *new expressions* whose syntax is the same as that given in the last section. The body of a behavior definition is a command. Note that the concurrent composition of commands is a command. The syntax of *behavior definitions* is as follows:

⟨*behavior definition*⟩ ::=
    def ⟨*beh name*⟩ (⟨*acquaintance list*⟩) [⟨*communication list*⟩]
        ⟨*command*⟩
    end def

Quite often the identifiers to be bound depend on the kind of communication or acquaintance list: for example, if a communication sent to a bank is a withdrawal request then the communication must also specify the amount to be withdrawn; but if the communication is a request to

show the balance, then it should not specify any amount. We follow the
variant record structure of Pascal [Wirth 1972] to deal with the variability
of the identifier bindings. Basically, we branch on the value of an identifier
called the *tag-field* and, depending on the value of the tag-field, different
identifier bindings are expected. The value of tag-field is called a *case label*.
Acquaintance lists and communication lists are both instances of *parameter
lists*. The syntax of the parameter lists is as follows:

$\langle parameter\ list \rangle$ ::= $\{id \mid \langle var\ list \rangle\} \mid \{ ,id \mid ,\langle var\ list \rangle \}^* \mid \epsilon$
    $\langle var\ list \rangle$ ::= case $\langle tag\text{-}field \rangle$ of $\langle variant \rangle^+$ end case
    $\langle variant \rangle$ ::= $\langle case\ label \rangle$: ($\langle parameter\ list \rangle$)

where *id* is an identifier, ϵ is an empty string (in case the parameter list
is empty), the *tag field* is an identifier, and the *case label* is a constant
(data-value). The example below illustrates the use of parameter lists. A
communication list in the behavior definition of a bank account is given.

```
case request of
    deposit        : (customer, amount)
    withdrawal  : (customer, amount)
    balance       : (customer)
end case
```

Thus a communication [*deposit, Joe, $50.00*], where *Joe* is the mail address
of some actor, would be an appropriate communication to send to a bank
account created using the above behavior definition.

Although we have avoided specifying any type structure in our programming language for the sake of simplicity, it is not difficult to do so: all we
would have to do is use type declarations with every identifier. *Static type
checking* could be performed when the code is compiled to make sure that
the identifiers are used correctly in the commands (with respect to their
types). For example, identifiers used as targets must have the type mail
address. *Dynamic type-checking* can be used whenever a new actor is actually created: it would check if the parameters are correctly instantiated.
Dynamic type-checking would also have to be used when a communication
is accepted. The syntax of commands is as follows:

$\langle command \rangle$ ::= if $\langle logical\ expression \rangle$ then $\langle command \rangle$
                    $\{$else $\langle command \rangle\}$ fi |
                become $\langle expression \rangle$ |
                $\langle send\ command \rangle$ | $\langle let\ bindings \rangle \{\langle command \rangle\}$
                $\langle behavior\ definition \rangle$ | $\langle command \rangle^*$

The syntax is for the most part quite obvious. Note that fi delimits if; it is used to avoid the so-called "dangling else" problem in nested if commands (where it is not clear which if command the else expression belongs to). In pseudo-code we avoid using fi, when this is unnecessary. We have already defined *behavior definitions* above. Note that the scope of an identifier bound by a behavior definition is lexical. The syntax for *send command* was given in the last section. It is simply:

$$\langle send\ command \rangle ::= \quad \text{send } \langle communication \rangle \text{ to } \langle target \rangle$$

where communication is a list of values and the target is an identifier bound to the mail address of an actor. *Let bindings* allow one to use an abbreviation for an expression. There is no mutual recursion unless new expressions are being bound; in the latter case, the actors created can know each other's mail addresses. The syntax for *let bindings* is as follows:

$$\langle let\ bindings \rangle ::= \text{let } id\ =\ \langle expression \rangle\ \{\ \text{and } id\ =\ \langle expression \rangle \}^*$$

We give only one example of a behavior definition in SAL to illustrate the flavor of the syntax. The code below is for an actor which behaves like a *stack-node* discussed in example 3.2.1.

```
def stack-node (content, link)
    [ case operation of
         pop: (customer)
         push: (new-content)
      end case]
if operation = pop ∧ content ≠ NIL then
    become forwarder (link)
    send content to customer
fi
if operation = push then
    let P = new stack-node (content, link)
    { become stack-node (new-content, P)}
fi end def
```

We assume NIL is a predefined value and SINK is the mail address of some actor. A node can be created by a *new* command of the form given below.

$$\text{let } p\ =\ \text{new } stack\text{-}node\ (\text{NIL, SINK})$$

The node created will subsequently serve as the receptionist for the stack since the mail address bound to p will always represent the mail address of the topmost node of the stack.

3.3.2   Act

The language *Act* is a sufficient kernel for the *Act3* language which is a descendant of *Act2* [Theriault 1983]. One basic distinction between *Act* and SAL is that the former uses a *keyword-based* notation while the latter uses a *positional* notation. The acquaintance list in *Act* is specified by using identifiers which match a pattern. The pattern provides for freedom from *positional* correspondence when new actors are created. Patterns are used in pattern matching to bind identifiers, and authenticate and extract information from data structures. The simplest pattern is a *bind pattern* which literally binds the value of an identifier to the value of an expression in the current environment. The syntax of pattern matching is quite involved and not directly relevant to the our purposes here. We therefore skip it.

When an actor accepts a communication it is *pattern-matched* with the *communication handlers* in the actor's code and dispatched to the handler of the pattern it satisfies. The bindings for the communication list are extracted by the pattern matching as well. We do not provide the syntax for expressions except to note that *new expressions* have the same syntax as the one given in Section 3.2, namely the keyword **new** followed by a behavior expression. The syntax of behavior definitions in *Act* programs is given below.

⟨behavior definition⟩ ::=
   (<u>Define</u> (<u>new</u> id { (<u>with</u> identifier ⟨pattern⟩) }*)
               ⟨communication handler⟩*)

⟨communication handler⟩ ::=
   (<u>Is-Communication</u> ⟨pattern⟩ <u>do</u> ⟨command⟩*)

The syntax of commands to create actors and send communications is the same in actor definitions as their syntax at the program level. The syntax of the *send command* is the keyword **send-to** followed by two expressions. The two expressions are evaluated; the first expression must evaluate to a mail address while the second may have an arbitrary value. The result of the send command is to send the value of the second expression to the target specified by the first expression.

⟨command⟩ ::= ⟨let command⟩ | ⟨conditional command⟩ |
           ⟨send command⟩ | ⟨become command⟩

⟨let command⟩ ::= (<u>let</u> (⟨let binding⟩$^+$) <u>do</u> ⟨command⟩*)

⟨let binding⟩ ::= (identifier expression)

⟨conditional command⟩ ::= (<u>if</u> ⟨expression⟩
           (<u>then</u> <u>do</u> ⟨command⟩*)
           (<u>else</u> <u>do</u> ⟨command⟩*))

⟨send command⟩ ::= (<u>send-to</u> ⟨expression⟩ ⟨expression⟩)

⟨become command⟩ ::= (<u>become</u> ⟨expression⟩)

The example of a stack-node definition from Section 3.2 is repeated below. Note the keywords in the acquaintance and communication lists. These keywords allow a free order of attributions when actors are created or when communications are sent. All the bindings we give are simple; in general the bindings can be restricted to complex patterns which allow authentication of the data by pattern matching.

```
(define (new stack-node (with content ≡c)
                        (with next-node ≡next))
   (Is-Communication (a pop (with customer ≡m)) do
      (if (NOT (= c empty-stack))
          (then (become forwarder (next))
                (send-to (m) (a popped-top (with value c)))))))
   (Is-Communication (a push (with new-content ≡v)) do
      (let ((x (new stack-node (with content c)
                              (with next-node next)))
       do (become (stack-node (with content v)
                              (with next-node x)))))))
```

Chapter 4

A More Expressive Language

In this chapter, we will define some higher-level constructs that make the expression of programs somewhat simpler. The purpose of this exercise is two-fold: first, we wish to build a somewhat richer language and second, we wish to illustrate the versatility of the constructs in a minimal actor language. For purposes of brevity, we will use SAL in simple examples. In more involved examples, we simply use pseudo-code. The issues discussed in this chapter include: developing a notation to represent functions whose arguments are supplied by communications from several different actors; the question of *delegation* which arises when determining the replacement actor requires communicating with other actors; the meaning and representation of *sequential composition* in the context of actor system; and lastly, the implementation of *delayed* and *eager* evaluation for arbitrary expressions. Our interest in delayed and eager evaluation strategies stems in part from the fact that these strategies provide an interesting way to demonstrate the utility of mapping values like numbers into a corresponding set of *built-in* actors.

4.1 Several Incoming Communications

One of the simplest questions one can ask is what the representation of functions of several different arguments is going to be. Recall that communications in the kernel language are defined as a list of values. If all the values needed to evaluate a function are to be received from the same actor and at the same time, then the evaluation of the function can be done directly by a single actor. In general, however, carrying out some computation may require values from different actors. An actor need not know who the sender of the communication it is currently processing is. Modelling the above situation requires using some special protocols. The specifics of the construction are dependent on the type of scenario in which the multiple inputs are required.

4.1.1   A Static Topology

There are two distinct possible scenarios for an actor representing a function of several arguments. If the sender of the values used for the arguments is irrelevant, then the actor simply *becomes* an actor which responds appropriately to the next incoming communication. If the senders are relevant but statically determined, as would be the case in a typical example in a *dataflow* language, then one can represent the function as a system of actors as follows: for communications from each of the different senders, a different actor would serve as the *receptionist*, and one actor would do the final function evaluation. Each receptionist buffers communications until it receives a *ready* communication from the *function-apply* actor, and then it sends the *function-apply* actor another communication together with its own mail address. The mail addresses serve to identify the sender. A concrete picture to help visualize a *function-apply* actor is an agent on an assembly line who is putting nuts and bolts together and needs one of each to arrive in order to fasten them before passing the result on. The receptionists act to buffer the nuts and bolts.

Consider the simple case of a *function-apply* actor which needs two inputs and sends the result to an actor at the mail address m, as shown in Fig. 4.1. We assume actors at mail addresses m_1 and m_2 act to buffer incoming arguments and are the *receptionists* for this system of three actors. The actor at m is an external actor. The program of an actor which collects the arguments and invokes the function f can be given as follows.

We give two mutually recursive definitions. Only one actor need be created using the *two-inputs-needed* definition. The behavior of this actor will be alternately specified by one or the other of the definitions. One observation that can be made is that the mutual recursion in the definitions is simply to make it easier to understand the code: It would be entirely possible to write a single definition to achieve the same purpose. The alternate definition would use an acquaintance and branch on its value to the two possible behaviors.

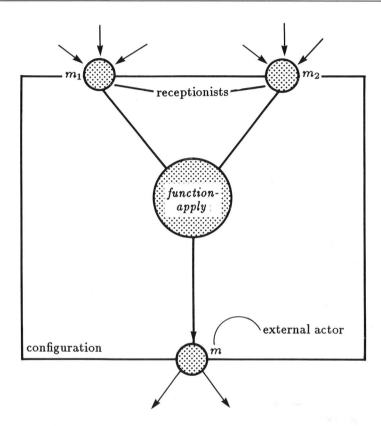

Figure 4.1: *A fixed topology for a two input function. The function-apply actor accepts communications from the actors m_1 and m_2 which serve as receptionists to the system and buffer incoming communications. Once function-apply has received the two arguments, it evaluates the function and sends the result to the actor m which is the future for some actor outside the system. (See Example 3.2.3 for external actors.)*

```
def two-inputs-needed (m₁ , m₂ , m) [ sender , arg ]
    if sender = m₁
        then become one-input-needed (m₁, m₂, second, arg)
        else become one-input-needed (m₁, m₂, first, arg)
    fi end def
```

> def *one-input-needed* (m_1, m_2, m, *new-arg-position*, *old-arg*)
> [*sender* , *new-arg*]
> let k = (if *new-arg-position* = *second* then f (*old-arg* , *new-arg*)
> else f (*new-arg* , *old-arg*) fi)
> { send [k] to m }
> send *ready* to m_1
> send *ready* to m_2
> become *two-inputs-needed* (m_1 , m_2)
> end def

A *function-apply* actor which needs two inputs from actors m_1 and m_2 can be created by the expression new *two-inputs-needed* (m_1, m_2).

4.1.2 A Dynamic Topology

A more interesting case of a many argument function is one in which the arguments are received from actors which are determined, or become known, dynamically. For example, more input may be needed during the course of computation from senders whose mail addresses were unknown to the actor computing the function. The mail address of such a sender may become known in the course of the computation since it can be received in a communication; this situation represents a dynamic topology on the interconnection network of actors. For example, an interactive program may need more input to continue with some transaction. The source of the input may vary and may be communicated in the course of the computation by some other actor (or by the programmer). A static topology in which all the communications are received from only those senders which were defined before the computation started will not work in this case. In fact the senders may not even exist at the start of the computation.

In the actor model, mail addresses of actors may be received in an incoming communication. These mail addresses can be used as targets for communications by the actor which receives them, a kind of dynamic reconfiguration that is not possible in dataflow systems. In this section, we extend the syntax of SAL to simplify expressing the need for more input. The general form for implementing requests for input from some particular actor is a *call expression* which may occur within the body of an actor. Call expressions have the following syntax:

$$\text{call } g\,[\,k\,]$$

where k is a communication and g is an identifier bound to a mail address. Note that g may be determined dynamically (i.e., at run-time). The value of the call expression is the communication sent by g as the *reply* to the

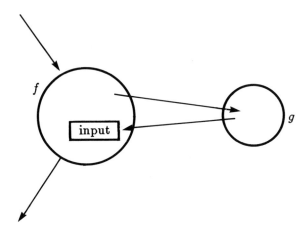

Figure 4.2: *The behavior of actor f in response to a communication may be a function of a communication from the actor g. The actor f may send a request to g for more input. Note that this picture is somewhat misleading because f need not wait for the reply from g; instead f will create a customer representing the continuation and send the mail address of the customer along with the request to g which will subsequently reply to the customer.*

present communication k. If the call expression occurs in the code for f, one can picture the flow of computation as in Fig. 4.2. However, the figure is somewhat misleading as a representation of what actually occurs in an actor system. The actor f does not (necessarily) have to wait for the reply from the actor g: a customer can be created which will continue processing when the *reply* from the actor g arrives. While the customer is "waiting" for the reply from g, the actor f may accept any communications pending in its queue.

The use of customers to implement *continuations* is more accurately portrayed in Fig. 4.3. This figure may be compared to the example of the recursive factorial in Section 3.2. There is sequentiality in some of the events that are triggered in the course of the computation initiated by a communication to the actor f. The sequentiality is modelled by the causality ordering on the events. However, other commands are executed concurrently. For example, if the call expression occurs in the following context in the code for f:

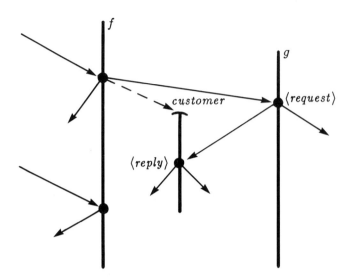

Figure 4.3: *The behavior of actor f is defined by program with a call ex-pression which requests more input. Some of the events are activated by the reply to a customer. The actor f simply creates a customer and may subsequently process other communications even as the customer waits for a reply from g.*

$$S'$$
$$\text{let } x = (\ \text{call } g\,[\,k\,]\ )\ \{S\}$$
$$S''$$

then the actions implied by S' and S'' can be executed concurrently with the request to g. Moreover, as discussed above, we do <u>not</u> force the actor f to wait until the reply from the actor g is received. The actor f would be free to accept the next communication on its mail queue, provided it can compute its replacement.[1] The customer created to carry out the actions implied by the command S will wait for the reply from the actor g.

Notice that the general scheme for representing requests is analogous to our earlier implementation of the factorial actor. Using a *call* expression, the program for a recursive factorial may be written as follows:

---

[1]We will discuss the case where an actor cannot compute its replacement without further input in the next section.

```
def exp Rec-Factorial ( ) [n]
    become Rec-Factorial ( )
    if n = 0
        then reply [1]
        else reply [n * (call self [n − 1])]
    fi
end def
```

We use def exp instead of def so that it is clear that the actor will return
a reply to a customer that is implicit in all communications accepted. Thus
a typical incoming communication sent to an expression actor has the form:

$$[\, m,\, k_1, \ldots, k_j \,]$$

where m is the mail address of the customer and $k_1, \ldots, k_j$ are the values needed to compute the expression. Our syntax explicitly shows only
$[k_1, \ldots, k_j]$; the mail address m is bound when the expression actor gets
a communication. A compiler can insert the customer and subsequently
map the command reply $[x]$ into the equivalent command:

$$\text{send } [\,x\,] \text{ to } m$$

The actor with the mail address m will be the customer which will continue
the transaction initiated at the time of its creation. Comparing the above
code with that of factorial in the previous chapter (see Fig. 3.4) should
make it clear how the behavior of the appropriate customer can be derived:
essentially, the segment of the environment which is relevant to the behavior
of the customer has to be preserved; this is done by dynamically creating a
customer. A SAL compiler whose target language is the kernel of SAL can
translate the above code to one in which the customer creation is explicit.
Also note that only one reply command may be executed (in response to a
single request).

Thus a purely expression oriented language can be embedded in SAL (or
equivalently in *Act*). The concurrency in such a language is inherent and
the programmer does not have to worry about the details related to creating
customers for implementing continuations. Because the programmer has no
direct access to the mail address of the customer created, another advantage
to the "automatic" creation of customers is that it provides protection
against improper use of the customer by the programmer.

There is one aspect of the expression oriented language that may be
disturbing to functional programming *aficionados*: namely, the presence
of side-effects implicit in the become command. Recall that the ability to

specify a replacement behavior is necessary to model objects with changing local states. The become command provides a mechanism to do so. The become command is actually somewhat analogous to recursive feedback in a dataflow language. This similarity (and the differences) will be discussed in greater detail in Chapter 6.

4.2   Insensitive Actors

When an actor accepts a communication and proceeds to carry out its computations, other communications it may have received must be buffered until the replacement behavior is computed. When such a replacement behavior is known, it processes the next communication in the mail queue. This may be one of the buffered communications or a newly accepted communication. The precise length of time it takes for an actor to respond to a communication is not significant because no assumption is made about the arrival order of communications in the first place.[2]

However, the desired replacement for an actor may depend on communication with other actors. For example, suppose a checking account has overdraft protection from a corresponding savings account. When a withdrawal request results in an overdraft, the balance in the checking account after processing the withdrawal would depend on the balance in the savings account. Thus the checking account actor would have to reply back to the savings account actor, and more significantly the savings account must communicate with the checking account, before the new balance (and hence the desired replacement behavior) is determined. Therefore the relevant communication from the savings account can <u>not</u> be buffered until a replacement is specified!

We deal with this problem by defining the concept of an *insensitive actor* which processes a type of communication called a *become communication*. A become communication tells an actor its replacement behavior. The behavior of an insensitive actor is to buffer all communications until it receives a communication telling it what to become. (Recall that *external declarations* were similarly implemented in Example 3.2.3.)

First consider what we would like the behavior of a *checking account* to be: if the request it is processing results in an overdraft, the checking account should request a withdrawal from the associated *savings account*. When a reply from the savings account is received by the checking account, the account will do the following:

---

[2]Communication delays are an important performance issue for a particular realization of the abstract actor architecture. Our focus here is restricted to semantic questions.

- Process requests it subsequently receives with either a zero balance or an unchanged balance; and,

- Reply to the customer of the (original) request which resulted in the overdraft.

Using a *call expression*, we can express the fragment of the code relevant to processing overdrafts as follows:

```
let r = (call my-savings [ withdrawal, balance − amount ] )
  { if r = withdrawn
       then become checking-acc ( 0, my-savings )
       else become checking-acc ( balance , my-savings )
    fi
    reply [ r ] }
```

To show how a call expression of the above sort can be expressed in terms of our kernel, we give the code for a bank account actor with over-draft protection. Again the code for the customers and the insensitive actors need not be explicitly written by the programmer but can instead be generated by a compiler whenever a call expression of the above sort is used. That is to say, if a become command is in the lexical scope of a *let expression* that gets its binding using a *call expression*, then the compiler should do the work explicitly given in the example below. Not requiring the programmer to specify the behavior of the various actors created, such as the insensitive bank account and the customer to process the overdraft, protects against erroneous communications being sent to these actors; it also frees the programmer from having to choose her own protocols.

A bank account with an overdraft protection is implemented using a system of four actors. Two of these are the actors corresponding to the checking and savings accounts. Two other actors are created to handle requests to the checking account that result in an overdraft. One of the actors created is simply a buffer for the requests that come in to the checking account while the checking account is *insensitive*. The other actor created, an *overdraft processor*, is a customer which computes the replacement behavior of the checking account and sends the reply to the customer of the withdrawal request. We assume that the code for the savings account is almost identical to the code for the checking account and therefore we do not specify it here. The structure of the computation is illustrated by Fig. 4.4 which gives the actor event diagram corresponding to a withdrawal request causing an overdraft.

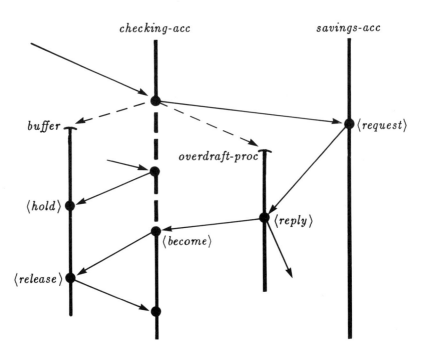

Figure 4.4: *Insensitive behaviors provide a mechanism for locking an actor. An insensitive actor continues to receive communications and may respond to some kinds of communications while buffering others. Specifically, during the dashed segment the insensitive checking account buffers any requests for checking transactions it receives.*

The behavior of the checking account, when it is not processing an overdraft, is given below. When the checking account accepts a communication which results in an overdraft, it becomes an insensitive account.

The behavior of an "insensitive" bank account, called *insens-acc*, is quite simple to specify. The insensitive account forwards all incoming communications to a buffer unless the communication is from the overdraft process it has created.[3] The behavior of a buffer is similar to that described in Example 3.2.3. The buffer can create a queue of communi-

---

[3]Due to considerations such as *deadlock*, one would program an insensitive actor to be somewhat more "active" (see Section 6.1). Good programming practice in a distributed environment require that an actor be *continuously available*. In particular, it should be possible to query an insensitive actor about its current status.

cations, until it receives a communication to forward the communications to some given actor. The buffer would then forward the buffered communications and become a forwarding actor so that any communications in transit will also get forwarded appropriately.

checking-acc (*balance* , *my-savings*) [⟨*request*⟩]
    if ⟨*deposit request*⟩ then
      become ⟨*checking-acc with updated balance*⟩
      send ⟨[*receipt*]⟩ to *customer*
    if ⟨*show-balance request*⟩
      send [*balance*] to *customer*
    if ⟨*withdrawal request*⟩ then
      if *balance* ≥ *withdrawal-amount*
        then become ⟨*checking-acc with updated balance*⟩
          send ⟨[*receipt*]⟩ to *customer*
        else let *b* = new *buffer*
          and *p* = new *overdraft-process* (*customer, self,*
              my-savings, balance)
          {become *insens-acc* (*b, p*)
          send ⟨[*withdrawal request with customer p*]⟩ to *my-savings*}

insens-acc (*buffer*, *proxy*) [*request* , *sender*]
    if *request* = become and *sender* = proxy
      then become ⟨*replacement specified*⟩
      else send ⟨*communication*⟩ to *buffer*

Finally, we specify the code for a customer to process overdrafts. This customer, called *overdraft-process*, receives the reply to the withdrawal request sent to the savings account as a result of the overdraft. The identifier *self* is always bound to the mail address of the actor itself (i.e., to the mail address of the actor whose behavior has been defined using the given behavior definition). The response from the savings account may be a *withdrawn*, *deposited*, or *complaint* message. The identifier *proxy* in the code of the insensitive account represents the mail address of the overdraft process. The proxy is used to authenticate the sender of any *become* message targeted to the insensitive actor.

overdraft-proc (*customer, my-checking, my-savings,*
             checking-balance) [⟨*savings-response*⟩]
send [⟨*savings-response*⟩] to *customer*
if ⟨*savings response is withdrawn*⟩
    then send [*become, checking-acc* (*0, my-savings*)] to *my-checking*
    else send [*become checking-acc* (*checking-balance, my-savings*)]
               to *my-checking*

4.3   Sequential Composition

In the syntax of our kernel language, we did not provide any notation for the sequential composition of commands. The omission was quite intentional. Although sequential composition is primitive to sequential machines, in the context of actors it is generally unnecessary. Recall that the primitive actor carries out only three sorts of actions: namely, sending communications, creating actors, and specifying a replacement behavior. The order of these actions is immaterial because there is no changing local state affecting these actions. Furthermore, the order in which two communications are sent is irrelevant: even if such an order was specified, it would not necessarily correspond to the order in which the communications were subsequently received.[4]

There are some contexts in which the order of evaluation of expressions is sequential even in the kernel of SAL. The two obvious places are *conditional expressions* and *let expressions*. A *conditional expression* in a conditional command must be evaluated <u>before</u> any of the commands in the chosen branch can be executed. Such evaluation cannot be done at compile time. However, the entire conditional command can be executed concurrently with any other commands at the same level. One can think of each command as an actor to which a communication is sent with the current bindings of the identifiers. The "command actor" in turn executes itself in the environment provided by the communication.

A *let command*, unless it is binding a *new expression*, is nothing more than an abbreviation that can be removed by the compiler if desired.[5] A compiler can substitute the expression for the identifier wherever the identifier is used (in the scope of the let binding).

A more interesting case is that of *let commands* binding *new expressions*. New expression bindings serve as abbreviations for actors rather than values. However, the behavior associated with an actor is not necessarily constant. For example, even though an identifier bound to a bank account refers to the same bank account, the behavior of the bank account is a function of the balance in it.

Let bindings have another characteristic: they may be mutually recursive since concurrently created actors may know of each other. The question arises: How can concurrently created actors affect each other's behavior? Concurrently created actors may know each other's mail address so that

---

[4]Unless the two communications are sent to the same target, the order in which they are received may simply depend on the viewpoint in which the determination is made. See the discussion in Section 2.2.

[5]In a higher-level language, a let binding may contain an expression which involves requests to other actors (i.e., may involve call expressions). In the previous section we showed how to translate such calls into the kernel language.

they can send each other communications. This in turn means that the mail addresses of each of the actors should be known before any of the actors are actually created since the behavior of each is dependent on the *other* actors' mail addresses. The operational significance of this is quite straight-forward.

Notwithstanding their absence in the kernel of our actor language, sequential composition of commands can be meaningful as a structural representation of certain patterns of computations. Sequential composition in these cases is the result of causal relations between events. For example, consider the commands S_1 and S_2 below:

$$S_1 \equiv \text{send } [\text{call } g\,[x]]\text{ to } f$$
$$S_2 \equiv \text{send } [\text{call } g\,[y]]\text{ to } f$$

then the sequential composition of S_1 with S_2 has a very different meaning than the concurrent composition of the two commands because the effect of accepting communication $[x]$ may be to change the actor g's subsequent behavior. Thus sequential composition can only result in some of the possible orders of events inherent in the concurrent composition.

Sequential composition is implemented using customers. The command $S \equiv S_1\,;\,S_2$ is executed concurrently with other commands at the same level. To execute S, the actions implied by the command S_1 are executed, including the creation of a customer to handle the reply from g. When this customer receives the reply from g, it carries out the other actions implied by S_1 as well as executing S_2.

Notice however that if S_1 and S_2 were commands to simply send communications to g, then no mechanism for any sequential composition of the two actions implied would be definable in our kernel language. Nothing signals the end of any action at an actor other than the causal relations in the events. For example, causality requires that the actions of an actor must follow the event that creates it. The conclusion to be drawn is that *concurrent composition* is intrinsic in a fundamental and elemental fashion to actor systems. Any *sequentiality* is built out of the underlying concurrency and is an emergent property of the causal dependencies between events occurring in the course of the evolution of an actor system.

4.4   Delayed and Eager Evaluation

In this section, we will develop a model of actors in which all expressions, commands and communications are themselves considered to be actors. We will call this model of actors the *universe of actors* model. The universe of actors model is useful for defining a language that is the actor equivalent of a purely expressional language. Specifically, the universe of actors model permits an easy (and efficient) implementation of the various expression evaluation mechanisms, such as *delayed* and *eager* evaluation, using message-passing.

Computation in actor systems is initiated by sending communications to actors that are *receptionists*. A single behavior definition in fact represents a specification of a system of actors with one of them as the receptionist for the system; the behavior of this receptionist is to execute a sequence of commands concurrently. We can consider each command to be an actor and the receptionist, upon accepting a communication, sends each command a message to execute itself with the current environment specified by the communication sent. The command will in turn send communications to expressions and create customers to process the replies. This process must, naturally, be bottomed out at some point by actors which do not send any "requests" to other actors but simply produce "replies." Hence, we need a special kind of actor, called a *built-in actor*, with the characteristic that some of these built-in actors need not (always) rely on more *message-passing* to process an incoming communication. Furthermore, built-in actors have a pre-defined behavior which never changes (i.e., the behavior is *unserialized*). Which actors are defined as built-in depends on the particular actor implementation.

4.4.1   Built-in actors

Built-in actors are used in order to "bottom-out" a computation.[6] The set of built-in actors may include the primitive data values and the basic operations on them. In particular, simple data objects such as integers, booleans and strings may be considered primitive. When an integer is sent a message to "evaluate" itself, it simply replies with itself. To carry out any computation efficiently, primitive operations such as addition must be pre-defined. There are various mechanisms by which a consistent model incorporating primitive operations can be developed; one such scheme is to also define operators such as addition to be built-in actors.

Our implementation encapsulates data values and the operations valid on the data into uniform objects. Hence, we define each integer as an actor which may be sent a *request* to add itself to another integer. The integer would then reply with the sum of the two integers. In fact an integer n may be sent a request to add itself to an arbitrary integer expression, e. In this case the request must also contain the local environment which provides the bindings for the identifiers in e. The bindings of the identifiers in the

---

[6]Theriault [Theriault 1983] used the term *rock-bottom actors* to describe these actors and the material on built-in actors closely follows his implementation in *Act2*.

local environment will be built-in actors; of course some of the bindings may be mail addresses of arbitrary actors. One way to understand this notion is to notice that the expression e is really equivalent to call e [env] where env is the environment in which the evaluation of the expression is to be performed. If e is an integer constant, it will reply with itself and, subsequently, n will reply with the correct sum. Specifically, the behavior of the integer n, in response to a request to add itself to the expression e in the environment env, can be described as:

$$\text{let } x = \text{call } e \; [\; env \;]$$
$$\{ \; \text{reply } [\; n + x \;] \; \}$$

If e is not an integer but an integer expression, a call to it must result in an integer. Thus the meta-circular behavior of the expression, $e \equiv e_1 + e_2$, is to send *evaluate* messages to each of the expressions e_1 and e_2 and to then send a message to the first expression (which would now have evaluated to the built-in actor that corresponds to the value of e_1) to add itself to the actor the second expression evaluates to.

Notice that we use integers and expressions as though they were identifiers bound to mail addresses, and indeed as actors they are. The distinction between identifiers and actors is similar to the distinction between numerals and numbers. In the universe of actors model, the *identifier* 3 is bound to the mail address of the *actor 3*. Since *3* is a built-in actor, its behavior is pre-defined. Furthermore, the behavior of the actor *3* never changes (such a behavior is called *unserialized*).

There may be more than one actor *3* in a program: the identifier 3 is completely local to the scope of its use. However, the identifier 3 has been reserved for a particular functional (unserialized) behavior and may not be used differently by the programmer. One useful implication of the fixed behavior of an integer like 3 is that it does not really matter how many 3's there are in a given actor system, or whether two 3's in an actor system refer to the same actor *3* or different ones. Ergo, when a communication contains the actor *3*, it is an implementation decision whether to copy the mail address of the actor *3* or whether to copy the actor itself. The latter possibility is useful for maintaining locality of reference in message-passing for efficiency reasons.[7] To put it another way, the unserialized nature of built-in actors implies that there is no theoretical reason to differentiate between the expression *new* 3, and simply 3.[8]

---

[7]There is no notion of *copying* actors in the actor model. What we mean is the creation of a new actor with a behavior identical to the current behavior of the (old) actor.

[8]Note that 3 denotes both a behavior and an actor.

4.4.2   Delayed Evaluation

In functional programming, *delayed evaluation* is useful for processing infinite structures by exploring at any given time, some finite segments of the structure. Using delayed expressions, the evaluation of a function is explicitly delayed until another function "resumes" it. Thus, delayed evaluation is the functional equivalent of co-routines [Henderson 1980].

In actor systems, it is *not* necessary to define delayed evaluation as a primitive: Since an actor acquires a replacement behavior as a result of processing a task, an actor already represents an infinite structure which unfolds one step at a time (in response to each communication accepted). Similarly, co-routines are one particular case of a concurrent control structure; actors allow one to define *arbitrary* concurrent control structures. Each control structure defines a graph of activations of processes and, as such, every control structure can be represented as a pattern of message-passing. The actor model allows dynamically evolving patterns of message-passing. Static control structures, such as co-routines, are a special (degenerate) case of the dynamic structures.

As the above discussion suggests, delayed evaluation is a *syntactic* extension to an actor language and <u>not</u> a *semantic* one. We define delayed expressions in order to make our purely expression oriented extension of SAL more expressive; the construct does not add any expressive power to the language (Recall that expressiveness refers to the ease with which something can be programmed, and expressive power refers to whether a computation can be at all carried out).

Let the expression delay e denote the mail address of the expression e as opposed to the actual value of e. Recall that the expression e is equivalent to call e [env] where [env] is the current local environment. The environment provides a closure which is retained so that later calls to the expression do not evaluate incorrectly.

For purposes of the discussion below, assume that the local environment in which identifier bindings are to be resolved is sent to any expression receiving an evaluation request. Now we have to decide what is meant by expressions which contain delayed expressions as subexpressions. For example, the expression :

$$e_1 \equiv e_2 \ * \ \text{delay} \ e_3$$

is a product of an arithmetic expression and a delayed (arithmetic) expression. When e_2 has been evaluated it receives the request [*, delay e_3], where delay e_3 represents the mail address of the expression e_3. Assume e_2 has evaluated to some integer n. There are two ways of handling this situation. One way is to "return" (i.e., to reply with) its current local state, which will be equivalent to the expression $n * e_3$. The other is to evaluate e_3 by sending it an eval message. In any event, e_1 *becomes* an actor behaviorally equivalent to the expression $n * e_3$, because the next time it is asked to evaluate itself, it will return the value of the product.

4.4.3 Representing Infinite Structures

The delayed expressions we have defined so far do not really represent potentially infinite structures, because the expressions they define are not recursive. However, our **def exp** behavior definitions already provide for such recursive structures. In this section we explore this analogy with the help of a detailed example. We will present an example using a functional programming notation and using actors. Two different actor systems are defined with equivalent observable behavior; the second system uses actors that change their behavior. Furthermore, the second actor system does not use the list construction and separation operators. Thus the flavor of the two actor systems is quite different even though they have similar behaviors.

The Example in Functional Programming

The purpose of the following example is to define some functions which evaluate a given number of initial elements of an infinite list. The notation uses a functional form for the *cons* operation but not for the *car* or *cdr*. All functions are taken from [Henderson 1980]. Consider the delayed expression in the function *integersfrom(n)* below:

$$integersfrom(n) \equiv cons(n \text{ , } \textbf{delay } integersfrom(n + 1))$$

integersfrom(n) is an example of such an infinite list, namely the list of all the integers greater than n. This list may be evaluated only partially at any given point in time. The function *first(i, x)* defined below gives the first k arguments for an infinite list x whose *cdr* has been delayed. (In functional programming, one has to explicitly *force* the evaluation of a delayed list.)

$$first(i, x) \equiv \text{if } i{=}0 \text{ then NIL}$$
$$\text{else cons (car } x, first (i - 1 \text{ , force cdr } x))$$

Now we define two more functions which can be used to return the cumulative sum of all the elements of a list up to some $i\underline{th}$ element. The function *sums(a, x)* returns a list whose $i\underline{th}$ element is the sum of the first i elements of the list x and the integer a. Finally, the function *firstsums(k)* uses the functions defined so far to return the list of initial sums of the first i positive integers.

$sums\,(a,x) \equiv$ cons $(a + $ car $x,$ delay$(\,sums\,(a + $ car $x,$ force cdr $x\,)\,)$
$firstsums\,(k) \equiv first\,(\,k,\,sums(0,\,integersfrom\,(1)))$

A System of Unserialized Actors

Let us now define an actor system which produces the same behavior. We will do this in two different ways. First, we define a system of actors all of whom have unserialized behaviors (i.e., they are always replaced by an identically behaving actor). The actors' behavior definitions do not contain any become commands because the default is that if no executable become command is found in the code of an actor, the actor is replaced by an identically behaving actor. We will subsequently define a system of actors which uses serialized behaviors when appropriate. The idea behind defining these two different but equivalent systems is to show the relation between actor creation and actor replacement. The systems also show the relation between *delay expressions* and actor creation.

Assume that the operations cons, car and cdr exist and are defined on actors representing *lists*. cons is sent the mail address of two actors and returns a list of the two mail addresses. It is important to note the equivalence of the mail address of a *built-in* actor and the actor itself. There are two possibilities for a list x: it may consist of a built-in actor (equivalently the mail address of a built-in actor) or it can be the mail address of an arbitrary list. car x equals x if x is a built-in actor, or equivalently the mail address of a built-in actor, otherwise car x is the mail address of the first element of the list. cdr x is NIL if x is a built-in actor, otherwise it returns a mail address corresponding to the rest of the list.

All the actors whose behavior is given by the code below are expressions. We will not bother to enclose the definitions in def exp $\cdots$ end def since the definitions are all rather brief. There is no need for *delay* or *force* operators: a delayed list is represented by the mail address of an actor representing that list. Forcing is implicit whenever a *call* is made to an expression.

The first function we define is *integersfrom(n)*. The behavior of an *integersfrom(n)* actor is that it responds to an *evaluate* request (i.e., a request of the form [ ]) by replying with a list whose car is the integer n and whose cdr is the mail address of an actor with the behavior *integersfrom(n+ 1)*.

$integersfrom(n)\,[\,]\equiv$ reply [cons $(n,$ new $integersfrom(n+1))\,]$

The behavior of an actor whose behavior is given by *first* ( ) is as follows: when it is sent a request $[i, x]$, where i is an non-negative integer and x is an arbitrary list, it replies with the first i elements of the list. We assume that the list x is sufficiently long to have i elements.

first( ) [*i,x*] ≡ if *i=0* then reply [NIL]
else reply [cons (car *x*, call *self* [*i* − 1, cdr *x*])]

Finally, we give the behavior definitions for the two remaining actors. *firstsums*( ) defines an actor whose behavior is to give a finite list whose *ith* element is the sum of the first *i* non-negative integers. The length of the list of sums in the reply is specified in the communication received. In order to create a system which returns the list of initial sums of non-negative integers, we need to create only a *firstsums*( ) actor; all the other actors will be created by this actor. The actor created will always be the sole receptionist for such a system since no mail address is ever communicated to the outside.

sums(*a, x*) [ ] ≡ let *b* = *a* + car *x*
{ reply [cons (*b* , new *sums* (*b*, cdr call *x*[ ]))] }

firstsums( ) [*k*] ≡ let *p* = new *integersfrom* (1)
and *s* = new *sums* (0, *p*)
and *f* = new *first*( )
{ reply[call *f* [*k, s*]] }

The fact that all the behaviors are unserialized implies that it is possible to use the same actors for different requests. Thus if an actor with behavior *first*( ) exists, it doesn't matter if a communication is sent to the same actor or to a new actor created with the behavior *first*( ). The converse of this property is that an actor with unserialized behavior can never be a *history-sensitive shared object*; this same limitation is applicable to any purely functional program.

A System With Serialized Actors

We now attack the same problem with actors that may change their local state: i.e., actors that may be replaced by actors whose behavior is different from their own. The point of defining this system is to show the relation between actor creation and behavior replacement. The example also illustrates the similarity between a *delayed expression* and an actor with a *serialized behavior*.

It should be noted that actors are in fact more general than expressions in functional programming. For one, actors, unlike expressions, may represent (history-sensitive) shared objects. For example, a bank account written as a function which returns a partly delayed expression will have returned an argument purely local to the caller. This means that such a bank account can <u>not</u> be shared between different users (or even between the bank manager and the account owner!). In some dataflow architectures, the problem of sharing is addressed by assuming a special *merge* element. However dataflow elements have a static topology (see the discussion in Chapter 2).

The definitions below do not use *cons*, *car*, and *cdr* operations. Instead we simply construct and bind the communication lists. The behavior definition of *integersfrom(n)* is that it accepts a simple evaluate message, [ ], and replies with the integer n. However, the actor presently *becomes* an actor with the behavior *integersfrom(n + 1)*. An actor with its behavior defined by *sums(a, x)* has two acquaintances, namely a and x. a is the sum of the first *umpteen* elements and x is the mail address of an actor which replies with the *umpteen*+1 element of the list. The *sums* actor calls x and replies with the next sum each time it is called.

The behavior definition of *first* is similar to the previous section except that we use explicit *call*'s. The definition of *firstsums( )* is identical to the one given above, and is therefore not repeated.

$integers\text{-}from(n)$ [ ] ≡ (reply [n]
$\qquad\qquad\qquad\qquad$ become $integers\text{-}from(n + 1)$))

$first(\ )$ $[i, x]$ ≡ if $i=0$ then reply [ ]
$\qquad\qquad\qquad$ else let $a =$ call x [ ]
$\qquad\qquad\qquad\qquad\qquad$ { reply [a, call $self$ $[i - 1, x]$] }

$sums(a, x)$ [ ] ≡ let $b = a +$ call x [ ]
$\qquad\qquad\qquad$ {reply [b]
$\qquad\qquad\qquad$ become $sums(b, x)$ }

The concept of *replacement* provides us with the ability to define *lazy evaluation* so that the same expression would not be evaluated twice if it were passed (communicated) unevaluated (i.e., if its mail address were sent). If lazy evaluation was desired, one could send communications containing the mail addresses of expressions, instead of the built-in actors the expressions would evaluate to. In this scheme, the message-passing discipline is equivalent to a *call-by-need* parameter passing mechanism, instead of a *call-by-value* which is the default in our definition of SAL.[9]

---

[9]Although "values" are passed in our primitive actor languages, it is important to note that often these values are the mail addresses of actors. In such cases the behavior of the system is similar to passing parameters using *call-by-reference*.

Object-oriented Code

It should be noted that we have given the code in a manner that makes it easy to compare the example in an actor language with the same example in a functional programming language. A more object-oriented way of coding the example would be by sending actors "car" and "cdr" messages instead of "applying" car or cdr to the replies received in response to an eval message. In the former case, the system is somewhat more modular.

The code for an unserialized version can be written as follows. Note that we use a case command instead of branching on conditionals when the use of the case command aids clarity.

$cons\,(first,\,rest)\,[msg] \equiv$
 case *msg* of
   car : reply $[first]$
   cdr : reply $[rest]$
 end case

$integersfrom\,(n)\,[msg] \equiv$
 case *msg* of
   car : reply $[n]$
   cdr : reply $[$ new $integersfrom\,(n+1)]$
 end case

$sums\,(a,\,x) \equiv$
 case *msg* of
   car : reply $[a]$
   cdr : reply $[$ new $sums\,(\,a + $ call $x\,[car],$ call $x\,[cdr]\,)]$
 end case

$first(\,)\,[i,\,x] \equiv$
 if $i = 0$
   then reply $[\,$NIL$\,]$
   else reply $[$ new $cons\,($ call $x\,[car],$ call $self\,[i-1,$ call $x\,[cdr]\,]\,)]$

The point of actor architectures is not so much to simply conserve computational resources but rather to provide for their greedy exploitation—in other words, to spread the computation across an extremely large-scale distributed network so that the overall parallel computation time is reduced. At the same time, it would be inadvisable to repeat the same computation simply because of the lack of the ability to store it—a serious problem in purely functional systems [Backus 1978]. In the next section we provide a strategy for evaluation of expressions which satisfies these requirements.

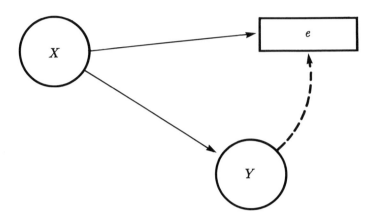

Figure 4.5: *Eager evaluation. The dotted line shows the acquaintance relation. X creates Y and tells it about e while concurrently sending an evaluate message to e. The expression actor e is called a future.*

4.4.4   Eager Evaluation

The inherent parallelism in actors provides many options for a greedy strategy in carrying out computations. The idea is to dynamically spawn numerous actors which will carry out their computations concurrently. These actors can exploit all the available resources in a distributed systems. We have already seen the use of pipelining of replacement actors as a mechanism for providing a greater potential for parallel execution, and thus increasing the speed of execution on a concurrent architecture. In an actor language, the pipelining is made possible by the use of customers in which *continuations* are incorporated as first-class objects.

Another mechanism by which the available parallelism in an actor language can be exploited is by schemes for *eager evaluation*. To speed up a computation to its logical limits, or at least to the limit of the number of available processes in a particular network, one can create an actor with the mail addresses of some expressions (which have not necessarily been evaluated) as its acquaintances. So far, this is similar to how one would implement *call-by-need*. However, for eager evaluation we concurrently send the expression, whose mail address is known to the actor created, a request to evaluate itself. Such an expression is an example of a *future* [Baker and Hewitt 1977]. Fig. 4.5 shows this pictorially. The net effect is that an actor *Y* which has been created may accept a communication even as the expression *e* which is its acquaintance is being evaluated concurrently. The expression subsequently *becomes* the actor it evaluates to. Thus the evaluation of the same expression need not be repeated.

Chapter 5

A Model For Actor Systems

A model for any collection of objects provides a map from the objects into equivalence classes which contain elements that are considered to be indistinguishable from each other. In other words, a *model* provides an abstract perspective in which the "irrelevant" details are ignored in establishing the equivalence of systems. In a *denotational model*, the meaning of a system can be derived from the meanings of its constituent parts. We will refer to this property as *compositionality*.

The semantics of sequential programming languages has been rather successful in building denotational models of programs which abstract away the *operational* details of the sequential systems defined by the programs. In the case of concurrent systems, however, the requirements of compositionality have resulted in proposed denotational models which retain substantial operational information. The reason for this is as follows. Composition in concurrent systems is achieved by interleaving the actions of the systems that are composed; thus the denotations for a system require the retention of information about the intermediate actions of the system (see for example [Milner 1980] or [deBakker and Zucker 1982]).

In this chapter we will develop a model for actor systems based on semantics by reductions. The actor semantics follows a structured operational style long advocated by Plotkin [Plotkin 1971]. In particular, we define transition relations which represent the evolution of an actor system as the computations it is carrying out are unfolded. Two transition relations are necessary to capture the behavior of an actor system. The first of these, called a *possible transition*, represents the possible orders in which the tasks may be processed. It turns out that the possible transition relation is insufficient to capture the guarantee of mail delivery. We therefore define a second transition relation, called *subsequent transition*, which expresses just such a guarantee.

The plan of this chapter is as follows. The first section specifies a formal definition for the configuration of an actor system and states the requirements relevant to defining an operational semantics for actors. In the second section we map actor programs to the initial configurations they define. The last section discusses two kinds of transition relations between configurations. These transition relations provide an operational meaning to actor programs.

5.1   Describing Actor Systems

A *configuration* of an actor system is described by the actors and tasks it contains. There is no implied uniqueness in the configuration of an actor system: different observers may consider the system to be in quite different configurations. This issue is discussed in greater detail in Section 5.3. To describe the actors in a system, we have to define their behaviors and their topology. Descriptions of actor systems are embodied in configurations. We first develop some notation to represent configurations. The definitions below assume that actor behaviors are well-defined—a topic we discuss in Section 5.2.

5.1.1   Configurations

A configuration of an actor system has two components: namely, the actors and the tasks. The tasks represent communications which are still pending; in other words, communications that have been sent but have not been processed by their targets. These communications may or may not have been delivered; in either case, they are yet to be processed. By specifying a unique tag for each task in a configuration, we keep equivalent tasks (i.e., tasks with the same communication and target) distinct.

Definition 5.1 Tasks. *The set of all possible tasks, T, is given by*

$$T = I \times M \times K$$

where I is the set of all possible tags, M is the set of all possible mail addresses, and K is the set of all possible communications. We represent tags and mail addresses as finite sequences of natural numbers, separated by periods, and communications as a tuple of values. If τ is a task and

$\tau = (t, m, k)$ *then we call* t *the* tag *for the task* τ, m *the* target, *and* k *the* communication.

We define a *local states function* to represent the behaviors of the actors from some viewpoint. Since there are only finitely many actors in any given configuration, this is really a partial function on the set of all possible mail addresses. However, when appropriate one can treat the *local states function* as a total function by defining an *undefined behavior*, called $\bot$, and mapping all undefined elements to $\bot$. For our immediate purposes, defining a total function is not necessary. In the definition below we assume that a set of possible actor behaviors $\mathcal{B}$ exists.

Definition 5.2 Local States Function. *A* local states function l *is a mapping from the mail addresses of the actors in a system to their respective behaviors, i.e.,*

$$l : M \longrightarrow \mathcal{B}$$

where M *is a finite set of mail addresses* $(M \subset \mathcal{M})$, *and* $\mathcal{B}$ *is the set of all possible behaviors, respectively.*

A configuration is defined below. A restriction on the tags of a configuration (specified in the definition below) is necessary to ensure that there always exist transitions from a given configuration with unprocessed tasks. We wish to avoid any tag conflicts as an actor system evolves.

Definition 5.3 Configurations. *A* configuration *is a two tuple* (l, T), *where* l *is a local states function and* T *is a finite set of tasks, such that:*

1. *no task in* T *has a tag which is the prefix of either another tag of a task in* T *or of a mail address in the domain of* l.[1]

2. *no mail address in the domain of* l *is the prefix of either another mail address in the domain of* l *or of a tag of a task in* T.

The degenerate case of the prefix relation is equality; thus no two tasks in a configuration may have the same tag. Thus the set T represents a function from a finite set of tags to the cross product of mail addresses and communications.

---

[1]The prefix relation is defined using the usual definition for strings. Note that we separate elements of the string using periods so that $t.1$ is not a prefix of $t.10$—the second elements of the two strings being distinct "letters" of the alphabet.

5.1.2   Requirements for a Transition Relation

What a behavior definition gives us is a map from a finite list of variables
to a behavior. These variables are given specific values whenever an actor
is created in the system. An actor's behavior specifies the creation of new
tasks and actors as a function of a communication accepted. Newly created
actors must have mail addresses that are unique and different tasks in a
system need to be kept distinct.

Although a global scheme for assigning mail addresses to newly created actors would provide a simple mechanism for generating new mail
addresses, in much the same way as the semantics of block declarations in
Pascal provides for the creation of new variables [deBakker 1980], such a
scheme is not a faithful representation of the concurrency inherent in an
actor system. We will instead provide a distributed scheme for generating
mail addresses.

One can maintain the uniqueness of tasks by providing distinct tags
for each and every task in an actor system. In fact, one purpose of mail
addresses is quite similar to that of tags: mail addresses provide a way of
differentiating between identically behaving actors. A network topology on
actors is given by a *directed graph* defined using the mail address of actors.
The nodes in such a graph denote the actors. An edge from an actor α to
an actor β means that β is an acquaintance of α.

We will use the unique tags of a task to define more unique tags and
mail addresses for the new tasks and actors created. Having defined a
scheme which guarantees the uniqueness of tags and mail addresses, we
can transform the instantiations of the behavior definition into a transition
function mapping a two-tuple of an actor and a task targeted to the actor
into a system of actors and tasks. This transition relation can be extended
meaningfully to a system of actors and tasks as long as mail addresses and
tags are generated in a distributed fashion and maintain their uniqueness
as the system evolves.

5.2   Initial Configurations

Our goal is to map actor programs into the initial configurations they
define. To do so, we will specify the meaning of constructs in an actor
program and show how to combine the meanings in order to map a program
to an initial configuration. We confine our consideration to minimal actor
languages such as the kernel of SAL and *Act* defined in Section 3.2. Since
all extended constructs are definabie in such minimal languages, and since
the kernel is much simpler than any expressive extension, such a restricted
focus is not only pragmatically desirable but theoretically sufficient.

5.2.1 Formalizing Actor Behaviors

The behavior of an actor was described informally in Section 2.1.3. In a nutshell, we can represent the behavior of an actor as a mapping from possible incoming communications to three tuples of new tasks, new actors, and a replacement behavior for the actor. We give a domain for actors below. Since the given domain of actor behaviors is recursive, it is not immediately obvious that the behavior of an actor is well-defined: We can deduce from a simple cardinality argument (following Cantor) that not all functions of the form in Definition 5.5 will be meaningful.

There are two ways to resolve the domain problem for actors. The first solution is to use Scott's theory of *reflexive domains* [Scott 1972] to map actor behaviors into an abstract, mathematically well-defined space of functions. Applying Scott's theory, each actor program denotes a value in the specified abstract space. The value is derived by repeatedly applying a function that represents a transformation corresponding abstractly to a step in a program's execution—until a *fixed-point* is reached. However, such valuations may or may not suggest a means of implementing an actor language.

In the denotational semantics of sequential programs, a major advantage of the fixed-point approach has been the ability to abstract away from the operational details of particular transitions representing intermediate steps in the computation. The sequential composition of the meanings of programs corresponds nicely to the meaning of the sequential composition of the programs themselves. This also implies that the meaning (value) of a program is defined in terms of the meaning of its subcomponents [Stoy 1977]. Furthermore, since sequential composition is the only operator usually considered in the case of deterministic, sequential programs, the fixed-point method is fully *extensional* [deBakker 1980].

Unfortunately, fixed point theory has not been as successful in providing extensional valuations of concurrent programs. Problems arise because of the requirements of compositionality: in a concurrent system the history of a computation cannot always be ignored. We will return to this topic in Chapter 7.

What we propose to do in this chapter is to provide a functional form for the behavior of an actor in a given program. Specifying the meaning of a program in these terms does not abstract all the operational details related to the execution of the code. The behavior of actors will in turn be used to define the initial configuration and the transitions between configurations of the system as it evolves. One can map the transition system into an abstract mathematical domain. In fact one can show that the computation paths defined using the transition relation specify an *infor-*

mation system as defined in [Scott 1982]. The representations are entirely *intentional* in character and thus provide constructive intuitions about the nature of computation in actor systems.

Note that the semantics of actor programs developed in this section is denotational because the meaning of a program is derived from the meaning of its constituent parts. We begin by defining actors and their behaviors.

Definition 5.4 Actors. *The set of all possible actors, $\mathcal{A}$, is given by*

$$\mathcal{A} = \mathcal{M} \times \mathcal{B}$$

where $\mathcal{M}$ is the set of all possible mail addresses (as above), and $\mathcal{B}$ is the set of all possible behaviors.

The tag of the task processed by an actor α is used to define new tags for the tasks and new mail addresses for the actors that are created by α as a result of processing the task. Notice that only a finite number of new tags and mail addresses need to be specified. A recursive domain for actor behaviors is given below.

Definition 5.5 Behaviors. *The behavior of an actor with mail address m is an element of $\mathcal{B}$, where*

$$\mathcal{B} = (\, \mathcal{I} \times \{m\} \times \mathcal{K} \longrightarrow F_s(\mathcal{T}) \times F_s(\mathcal{A}) \times \mathcal{A} \,)$$

$F_s(\mathcal{T})$ is the set of all finite subsets of $\mathcal{T}$ and $F_s(\mathcal{A})$ is the set of finite subsets of $\mathcal{A}$. Furthermore, let β be a behavior for an actor at mail address m, and t be the tag and k be the communication of the task processed, such that $\beta(k) = (T, A, \gamma)$, where

$$T = \{\tau_1, \cdots, \tau_n\}$$
$$A = \{\alpha_1, \cdots, \alpha_{n'}\}$$

then the following conditions hold:

1. *The tag t of the task processed is a prefix of all tags of the tasks created:*

$$\forall i \, (1 \leq i \leq n \Rightarrow \exists m_i \in \mathcal{M} \, \exists k_i \in \mathcal{K} \, \exists t_i' \in \mathcal{I} \, (\tau_i = (t.t_i', m_i, k_i)))$$

2. *The tag t of the task processed is a prefix of all mail addresses of the actors created:*

$$\forall i \, (1 \leq i \leq n' \Rightarrow \exists \beta_i \in \mathcal{B} \, \exists t_i' \in \mathcal{I} \, (\alpha_i = (t.t_i', \beta_i)))$$

3. *Let I be the set of tags of newly created tasks and M be the set of mail addresses of newly created actors. Then no element of $I \cup M$ is the prefix of any other element of the same set.*

4. *There is always a replacement behavior.*

$$\exists \beta' \in \mathcal{B} \, (\gamma = (m, \beta'))$$

The example below is for illustrative purposes. The meaning developed in Section 5.2.2 will allow us to derive from the code the functional form given below.

Example 5.2.1 Recursive Factorial. The recursive factorial discussed in Section 2 is an example of an actor with unserialized behavior. The code for such an actor is given in Section 3.3. The behavior of a recursive factorial actor at the mail address m, (m, φ), can be described as follows:

$$\varphi(t, m, [k_1, k_2]) =$$
$$\begin{cases} \langle \{(t.1, k_2, [1])\}, \emptyset, (m, \varphi) \rangle & \text{if } k_1 = 0 \\ \langle \{(t.1, m, [k_1 - 1, t.2])\}, \{(t.2, \psi_{k_2}^{k_1})\}, (m, \varphi) \rangle & \text{otherwise} \end{cases}$$

where m is the mail address of the factorial actor, t is the tag of the task processed. The behavior of the newly created *customer* can be described as:

$$\psi_{k_2}^{k_1}(t', t.2, [n]) = \langle \{(t'.1, k_2, [n * k_1])\}, \emptyset, (t.2, \beta_\perp) \rangle$$

where $t.2$ is the mail address of the newly created actor, and t' is the tag of the task it processes. $\beta_\perp$ is *bottom-behavior*, which is equivalent to an infinite sink. It can be shown that in any actor system this newly created actor will receive at most one communication; thus the behavior of its replacement is actually irrelevant.

5.2.2   The Meaning of Behavior Definitions

Recall that an actor machine embodies the current behavior of an actor. Conceptually, each time a communication is processed by an actor, a new actor machine is created to accept the next communication. If the actor's behavior doesn't change as a result of processing a communication, the replacement machine is identical to the one it replaces. The behavior of an actor machine is quite simple: it involves no iteration, recursion, synchronization, or state change. The behavior is simply a function of the incoming communication and involves sending more communications to specified targets, creating new actors, and specifying a replacement actor machine.[2] We

---

[2]The rest of this section is a technical justification for a well-formed interpretation of actor behaviors and may be skipped without loss of continuity.

will use the syntactic default in an actor program that whenever there is no *become* command in the code of an actor, the replacement behavior is simply identical to the original behavior. One can now safely assert that all actors definable in an actor language like SAL specify a replacement behavior. Alternately, we could have decided that a behavior definition which did not provide a replacement in some cases was simply meaningless.

In this section, we closely follow the relevant notation and terminology from [deBakker 1980]. Each actor program consists of a finite number of behavior definitions which will form templates for all the behaviors of actors that may be created in the course of program execution. We will define the meaning of a behavior definition as a map from:

- the mail address, *self*, of the actor whose behavior has been defined using the template; and,

- the variables in the acquaintance list of the behavior definition.

And a map to a function mapping a task with target *self* into a three tuple consisting of:

- a set of tasks;

- a set of three tuples consisting of a mail address, a behavior definition and a list of values; and,

- a three tuple consisting of the mail address *self*, a behavior definition and a list of values.

We carry out the construction formally. We first define a syntax for the class of *primitive* expressions. There are three kinds of primitive expressions: integer, boolean, and mail address expressions. These expressions will occur in different commands. The class *Icon* typically corresponds to constant identifiers such as $3, 4, -1, \ldots$, while the class *Ivar* corresponds to the identifiers used for integers in a program. Note that there is no class of mail address constants in the expressions of our language because the programmer has no direct access to mail addresses. The primitive expressions given below are purely syntactic objects which will be mapped into mathematical objects by a valuation function.

Definition 5.6 Syntax of Primitive Expressions.

1. *Let Ivar, with typical elements $x, y, \ldots$, be a given subset of the class of identifiers, and Icon be a given set of symbols with typical elements $n, \ldots$. The class Iexp, with typical elements $s, \ldots$, is defined by*

$$s ::= x \mid n \mid s_1 + s_2 \mid \cdots$$

(Expressions such as $s_1 - s_2$ may be added.)

2. *Let Mvar, with typical elements $a, \ldots$, be a given subset of the class of identifiers, E be an element of Dvar (defined later) and $e_1, \ldots, e_i$ be arbitrary expressions, then the class Mexp, with typical elements $h, \ldots$, is defined by*

$$h ::= a \mid \mathsf{new}\ E(e_1, \ldots, e_i)$$

3. *Let Bvar, with typical elements $b, \ldots$, be a given subset of the class of identifiers, and Bcon be the set of symbols $\{\underline{\mathtt{true}}, \underline{\mathtt{false}}\}$. The class Bexp, with typical elements $b, \ldots$, is defined by*

$$b ::= \underline{\mathtt{true}} \mid \underline{\mathtt{false}} \mid s_1 = s_2 \mid h_1 = h_2 \mid \neg b \mid \cdots$$

We now assume the existence of three classes of mathematical objects: namely, a class of integers, V, a class of mail addresses, M, and a class of truth values, $W = \{tt, ff\}$. The integers and the truth values have the usual operations associated with them, such as addition for integers. We assume that the concatenation operator works for the mathematical objects called mail addresses since the class of mail addresses will be identical to the class of tags and the latter will be suffixed to define new mail addresses.

Let the set of primitive variables, *Pvar*, be the separated sum of integer, boolean, and mail address variables.[3] Similarly, let P be the set of primitive values representing the separated sum of the integers, the truth values, and the mail addresses. A *local environment* is defined as an element of:

$$\Sigma : Pvar \rightarrow Pval$$

There are three semantic functions that need to be defined to give a meaning to primitive expressions. Given a local environment, these functions map primitive expressions to primitive values:

$$
\begin{aligned}
\pi_1 &: Iexp &\rightarrow& \;(\Sigma \rightarrow V\;) \\
\pi_2 &: Bexp &\rightarrow& \;(\Sigma \rightarrow W\;) \\
\pi_3 &: Mexp &\rightarrow& \;(\Sigma \rightarrow M\;)
\end{aligned}
$$

The first two functions are defined by induction on the complexity of the arguments and have nothing to do with actor semantics in particular. We therefore skip them. We will define the meaning function below which

---

[3] Strictly speaking the sets *Bvar* and *Ivar* are superfluous since boolean and integer expressions can be defined without them. Given a single predefined behavior, actors can be constructed to represent integers or booleans. However, we will assume that all three kinds of variables exist and are distinct.

will provide the valuation for *new expressions*. Essentially, new expressions evaluate to a new mail address. We will assume that a single function π represents the separated sum of the three functions given above; thus π maps each expression into its corresponding value, given a particular local environment σ.

We now give the syntax of commands and behavior definitions. The syntactic classes defined are called *Cmnd* and *Bdef*. The syntax below is a slightly abbreviated form of SAL. The two noteworthy differences between SAL and the syntax are as follows. First, we allow let bindings only for *new expressions*. The semantics of let bindings in other cases is quite standard, and in any case not absolutely essential to actor programs. Second, we use *behavior expressions*, as opposed to arbitrary expressions, in *become commands*. A behavior expression is an expression which evaluates to a behavior. In our syntax, a behavior expression is an identifier bound to a behavior definition together with expressions which provide bindings for the acquaintances.

Definition 5.7 Syntax of Behavior Definitions.

1. *The class Cmnd with typical elements $S, \cdots$, given by*

   $$S ::= S_1//S_2 \mid \text{if } b \text{ then } S_1 \text{ else } S_2 \text{ fi} \mid$$
   $$\text{send } [e_1, \ldots, e_i] \text{ to } a \mid \text{become } E(e_1, \ldots, e_i) \mid$$
   $$\text{let } a_1 = \text{new } E_1(e_1, \ldots, e_{i_1}) \text{ and } \ldots$$
   $$\text{and } a_j = \text{new } E_j(e_1, \ldots, e_{i_j}) \ \{ \ S \ \}$$

   where the use of the identifiers corresponds to their reserved status above. The identifiers $E, \ldots$, are used as defined below.

2. *Let Dvar be the set of pre-defined symbols with typical elements $E, \ldots,$. The class Bdef with typical elements $D, \ldots$, is given by*

   $$D ::= \text{def } E(p_1, \ldots, p_i)[p'_1, \ldots, p'_j] \ S \ \text{enddef}$$

The semantics of the class *Cmnd* is defined below. The semantics maps a given local environment into a three tuple representing tasks created, actors created and a replacement behavior, respectively. Note that actors are denoted by a structure consisting of three components: namely, a mail address, an element of *Dvar*, and a list of primitive values which will map into the primitive variables used in the behavior definition using the element of *Dvar*. We also assume that two primitive variables, namely *self* and *curr*, of the class *Mvar* are defined by the local environment. *self* represents the mail address of the actor whose code contains the given command and *curr* represents the tag of the task being currently processed. The meaning function is defined on the complexity of the commands. We will not give the details of a complexity measure for the commands but will simply follow their syntactic definition. The details are trivial. Note that σ represents the local environment and $\sigma[\![a/x]\!]$ represents the environment which is equal to σ except for the fact that it binds the primitive value a to the primitive variable x. The operation $\uplus$ represents a component-wise union (i.e., the three components are "unioned" independently).

The meaning function $\mathcal{F}$ maps each command in a given local environment to a three tuple representing the communications sent, the actors created and the replacement actor. The meaning of concurrent commands is the component-wise union of the commands themselves, i.e., the communications sent are the communications sent by each, and the actors created are the union of the actors created by executing each of the commands. Recall that there may be only one executable become command in the code of an actor for any given local environment. If the union ends up with more than one replacement actor then it does not define an actor behavior. The main point of interest in concurrent composition is the suffixing of the current tags. This mechanism ensures that the new actors and tasks created by the actor will satisfy the prefix condition in Definition 5.5. Assume that *curr* is initially bound to t on the left hand side of all the equations given below.

$$\mathcal{F}(S_1//S_2)(\sigma[\![t/curr]\!]) = \mathcal{F}(S_1)(\sigma[\![t.1/curr]\!]) \uplus \mathcal{F}(S_2)(\sigma[\![t.2/curr]\!])$$

The meaning of the *conditional command* and the *send command* is straightforward. The *become command* specifies the replacement behavior by specifying an identifier which will denote a behavior definition and a list of values which will partially determine the local environment in which the command in the definition is executed. Note that tt represents the truth value true.

$$\mathcal{F} \text{ (if } b \text{ then } S_1 \text{ else } S_2 \text{ fi) } (\sigma) = \left\{ \begin{array}{ll} \mathcal{F}(S_1)(\sigma) & \textit{if } \pi(b) = \text{tt} \\ \mathcal{F}(S_2)(\sigma) & \textit{otherwise} \end{array} \right.$$

$$\mathcal{F}(\text{send } [e_1, \ldots, e_i] \text{ to } a)(\sigma[\![t/curr]\!]) = \\ \langle \{t.1, \pi(a)(\sigma), [\pi(e_1)(\sigma), \ldots, \pi(e_i)(\sigma)]\}, \emptyset, \emptyset \rangle$$

$$\mathcal{F}(\text{become } E(e_1, \ldots, e_i))(\sigma[\![m/self]\!]) = \\ \langle \emptyset, \emptyset, \{(m, E(\pi(e_1)(\sigma), \ldots, \pi(e_i)(\sigma)))\} \rangle$$

The creation of new actors is accomplished by *new expressions* and *let bindings*. We have to specify the new mail addresses for all concurrently created actors which may know each other's mail address. The command in the scope of the bindings is also executed in a local environment where all the identifiers for the actors are bound to the mail addresses of the newly created actors.

$$\mathcal{F}(\text{let } a_1 = \text{new } E_1(e_1, \ldots, e_{i_1}) \text{ and } \ldots \text{ and}$$
$$a_j = \text{new } E_j(e_1, \ldots, e_{i_j}) \ \{S\})(\sigma[\![t/curr]\!]) = \ \mathcal{F}(S)(\sigma') \uplus$$
$$\langle \emptyset, \{\alpha_n : \forall 1 \leq n \leq j(\alpha_n = (t.n, E_n(\pi(e_1)(\sigma'), \ldots, \pi(e_{i_n})(\sigma'))))\}, \emptyset \rangle$$

where $\sigma' = \sigma[\![a_1/t.1, \ldots, a_j/t.j]\!]$.

Now the meaning of a behavior definition is simply to extend a *program environment* by mapping each element of *Dvar* used in a behavior definition specified in the program into the meaning of the command contained in the behavior definition. We skip the (simple) proof that a behavior definition defines behaviors that satisfy the requirements of Definition 5.5. The tag and mail address generation schemes we used were intended to satisfy these requirements. The only other constraint of interest is that there be at most one executable become command. A behavior definition is simply not well-defined if its meaning violates this constraint.[4]

5.2.3 Mapping Actor Programs

The basic syntax of a SAL program consists of *behavior definitions* and commands. The commands are used to create actors and to send them communications.[5] Now a program environment associates the identifiers in *Dvar* with the meaning of commands for each behavior definition in the program. All other members of *Dvar* are undefined and may not be used in the commands of a syntactically correct program. The program contains a single command (recall that the concurrent composition of commands is a command) and its meaning is given using the function $\mathcal{F}$ defined above with the program environment as the local environment. The technique used here is similar to that in used in [deBakker 1980] where procedure variables are defined in the denotational semantics of recursion. The syntax of a program can be given as follows:

$$P ::= D_1 \ldots D_n \ S$$

---

[4] In an implementation, we would generate an error message.

[5] We are ignoring for the present the receptionist and external actor declarations; although such declarations are useful for imposing a modular structure on the programs, they do not directly affect transitions internal to the system.

where the D_i's represent behavior definitions and S represents a command (which may, of course, be the concurrent composition of other commands). The variable *curr* is initially bound to 1.

Note that none of the top level commands can be a become command because these commands are not being executed by an actor within the system. Thus an actor program is mapped into a two tuple representing the initial configuration. A transition relation tells us how to proceed from a given configuration by, nondeterministically,[6] removing a task from the system and adding the effects of processing that task. The effects of processing a task are given by the behavior of its target, which responds by creating actors and tasks and specifying a replacement behavior.

5.3 Transitions Between Configurations

In a sequential machine model, the intuition behind transitions is that they specify what actions might occur "next" in a system. However, in the context of concurrent systems, there is generally no uniquely identifiable transition representing the "next" action since events occurring far apart may have no unique order to them. Our *epistemological* interpretation of a transition is <u>not</u> that there really is a unique transition which occurs (albeit nondeterministically), but rather that any particular order of transitions depends on the *frame of reference*, or the *viewpoint*, in which the observations are carried out. This difference in the interpretation is perhaps the most significant difference between a *nondeterministic sequential process* and the model of a truly *concurrent system*: In nondeterministic sequential processes, a unique transition in fact occurs, while in concurrent systems, many transition paths representing different viewpoints may be consistent representations of the actual evolution.

Our justification for using a transition system is provided by the work of Clinger which showed that one can always define a (non-unique) *global time* to represent the order of events [Clinger 1981]. Events in Clinger's work were assumed to take infinitesimal time and the *combined order* of events was mapped into a linearly ordered set representing a global time. A global time is an order of events corresponding to the order in which some (purely conceptual) observer could record the events. Equivalently, a global time represents a linear order on events in the universe such that the order satisfies requirements of causality and is consistent with the local times of all actors in the universe.

Remark. Transitions, unlike events, may take a specific finite duration

---

[6]We will return to the issue of the guaranteeing mail delivery in Section 5.3.

and may therefore overlap in time. This is not a problem in actor systems because of the following reasons:

1. All transitions involve only the acceptance of a communication.

2. There is arrival order nondeterminism in the order in which communications sent are accepted and this arbitrary delay subsumes the precise duration of a transition. Specifically:

   (a) Precisely when a particular communication is sent because of a transition need not be explicitly modelled: Although a communication may not have been sent before another transition occurs, this possibility is accounted for by the fact that the communication sent may not cause the "next" transition.

   (b) When a replacement accepts the next communication targeted to the actor is indeterminate; thus the time it takes to designate the replacement need not be explicitly considered.

   (c) The above reasoning holds for creation of new actors as well.

Global time in any concurrent system is a *retrospective* construct: it may be reconstructed after the fact (although not as a *unique* linear order) by studying the relations on the events in a parallel system. It turns out that in implementations supporting actor systems, information about the order of events in a circumscribed system is often useful; it helps delimit *transactions*. Transactions are defined by the events affecting the reply to a given request (in particular, the events ordered between the request and its corresponding reply). Transactions are useful tools for debugging a system or allocating resources to sponsor activity. The determination of an order of events (the so-called *combined order* as it combines the arrival order with the order of causal activations) in an implementation is achieved by running the actor system in a special mode where each actor records events occurring at that actor and reconstructing the causal activations by following the communications sent.

The possible ways in which a conceptual observer records events, i.e., the behavior of such an observer, corresponds to that of some nondeterministic sequential process. This correspondence is the reason why nondeterminism is used in mathematical models to capture the parallelism. However, the character of the correspondence is *representationalistic*, not *metaphysical*. In particular, the behavior of a parallel system may be represented by many (consistent) nondeterministic sequential processes corresponding to different observers.

5.3.1   Possible Transitions

In this section, we discuss how actor systems may evolve in terms of their descriptions. A transition relation specifies how one configuration may be replaced by another that is the result of processing some task in the former.

Notation. Let *states* and *tasks* be two functions defined on configurations that extract the first and second components of a configuration, respectively. Thus the range of *states* is the set of local states functions and the range of *tasks* is the power set of tasks, where the set of tasks may be treated as a function from tags to target and communication pairs.

The definition for the possible transition relation essentially shows how an interpreter for an actor language would theoretically work. It thus specifies an operational semantics for an abstract actor language. Note that defining a language in this manner amounts to specifying its semantics by reduction. We will first define the possible transition relation and then show that such transitions do indeed exist for an arbitrary configuration.

Definition 5.8 Possible Transition. *Let c_1 and c_2 be two configurations. c_1 is said to have a possible transition to c_2 by processing a task $\tau = (t, m, k)$, symbolically,*

$$c_1 \xrightarrow{\tau} c_2$$

if $\tau \in tasks(c_1)$, and furthermore, if $states(c_1)(m) = \beta$ where

$$\beta(t, m, k) = \langle T, A, \gamma \rangle$$

and the following hold

$$
\begin{aligned}
tasks(c_2) &= (tasks(c_1) - \{\tau\}) \cup T \\
states(c_2) &= (states(c_1) - \{(m, \beta)\}) \cup A \cup \{\gamma\}
\end{aligned}
$$

Given a configuration and a task in it, there exists a possible transition from the configuration which is the result of processing the task. In order to prove this result, we need to show that a valid configuration can always be specified using the above equations for *tasks* and *states*. The proof of this proposition uses the fact that, in the initial configuration, tags and tasks are <u>not</u> prefixes of each other to prove that the same conditions are satisfied by the *tasks* and *states* of the configuration resulting from the transition. Note that a corollary of the condition that mail addresses are not prefixes of each other is that *states* is a function.

Let c_1 be a configuration and $\tau \in tasks(c_1)$. Let c_2 be the configuration obtained by processing τ, i.e. $c_1 \xrightarrow{\tau} c_2$, then the following lemmas hold.

Lemma 5.1 *No task in c_2 has a tag which is the prefix of the tag of another task in c_2.*

Proof. (By Contradiction). Let t_1 and t_2 be the tags of two tasks τ_1 and τ_2 in the configuration c_2 such that $t_1 = t_2.w$ for some string of integers w separated by periods. We examine the four possible cases of whether each of the tasks belongs to the configuration c_1.

If $\tau_1, \tau_2 \in tasks(c_1)$ then since c_1 is a valid configuration, we immediately have a contradiction. On the other hand, if neither of the two tasks are in c_1, then by Definition 5.5 the the prefix relation is not valid either.

We can therefore assume that one of the tasks belongs to the tasks of c_1 and the other does not. Suppose $\tau_1 \in tasks(c_1)$ and $\tau_2 \notin tasks(c_1)$. Since $\tau_2 \notin tasks(c_1)$, τ_2 has been created as a result of the transition. Thus $\exists i\,(t_2 = t.i)$, where t is the tag of the processed task τ. Together with the hypothesis that $t_1 = t_2.w$, this implies that $t_1 = t.i.w$. But since $\tau_1, \tau \in tasks(c_1)$ we have a contradiction to the prefix condition in the tasks of configuration c_1.

The only remaining case is that of $\tau_2 \in tasks(c_1)$ and $\tau_1 \notin tasks(c_1)$. Now $t_1 = t.i = t_2.w$. If w is an empty string then t is a prefix of t_2 and both are elements of $tasks(c_1)$, a contradiction. If $w = i$ then $t = t_2$ and thus τ_2 and τ have the same tag and they are both in $tasks(c_1)$, a contradiction. But if w is longer then a single number than t is a prefix of t_2 which also contradicts the condition that they are both tags of tasks in c_1. $\dashv$

Lemma 5.2 *No mail address of an actor in c_2 is the prefix of the mail address of another actor in c_2.*

Proof. We denote the prefix relation by $\preceq$. Let $\alpha_1 = (m_1, \beta_1)$ and $\alpha_2 = (m_2, \beta_2)$ be two actors in c_2. If α_1, α_2 are in c_1 then by Definition 5.3 we have a contradiction to the fact that c_1 is a valid configuration. Therefore at least one of α_1, α_2 is newly created. Without loss of generality, suppose α_2 is newly created.

By Definition 5.5(3), α_1 cannot also be a newly created actor. Thus $\alpha_1 \in states(c_1)$. Let t be the tag of the task τ. Since α_2 is a newly created actor, $m_2 = t.i$ for some nonnegative integer i. If $m_2 \preceq m_1$ then $t.i \preceq m_1$. But this implies $t \preceq m_1$, a contradiction to the fact that t is the tag of a task in c_1 and m_1 is the mail address of an actor in c_1. If $m_1 \preceq m_2$ then $m_1 \preceq t.i$. Now either $m_1 \preceq t$ or $m_1 = t.i$ in which case $t \preceq m_1$. In either case, we again have a contradiction to the fact that t is the tag of a task in c_1 and m_1 is the mail address of an actor in c_1. $\dashv$

The following two lemmas can also be proved similarly. The proofs are straightforward and are skipped.

Lemma 5.3 *The tag of a task in c_2 is not a prefix to the mail address of any actor in c_2.*

Lemma 5.4 *The mail address of an actor in c_2 is not a prefix to the tag of any task in c_2.*

The above lemmas imply the following theorem.

Theorem 5.1 *If c_1 is a configuration and $\tau \in tasks(c_1)$ then there exists a configuration c_2 such that $c_1 \xrightarrow{\tau} c_2$.*

5.3.2 Subsequent Transitions

Of particular interest in actor systems is the fact that all communications sent are subsequently delivered. This *guarantee of mail delivery* is a particular form of *fairness*, and there are many other forms of fairness, such as extreme fairness [Pnueli 1983], and fairness over arbitrary predicates. We will not go into the merits of the different forms here but will consider the implications of guaranteeing the delivery of any particular communication even when there is a possible infinite sequence of transitions which does not involve the delivery of a particular communication sent. To deal with the guarantee of mail delivery, it is <u>not</u> sufficient to consider the transition relation we defined in the last section. We will instead develop a second kind of transition relation which we call the *subsequent transition*. The subsequent transition relation was developed in [Agha 1985].[7] We first define a possibility relation as the transitive closure of the possible transition and then use it to define *subsequent transitions*.

Suppose the "initial" configuration of an actor system had a factorial actor and two requests with the parameters n_1 and n_2 respectively, where n_1 and n_2 are some nonnegative integers. Because there are two tasks to be processed in this configuration, there are two *possible* configurations that can follow "next." Each of these has several possible transitions, and so on. This motivates the definition of a fundamental relation between configurations which can be used to give actors a fixed-point semantics.[8] For a lucid exposition of fixed-point semantics see [Scott 1972].

---

[7]Milner brought to our attention that the relation we define here is similar to that developed independently in [Costa and Stirling 1984] for a *fair* Calculus of Communicating Systems.

[8]Such a domain does not respect fairness.

Definition 5.9 Possibility Relation. *A configuration c is said to possibly evolve into a configuration c', symbolically $c \longrightarrow^* c'$, if there exists a sequence of tasks, $t_1, \ldots, t_n$, and a sequence of configurations, $c_0, \ldots, c_n$, for some n, a non-negative integer, such that*

$$c = c_0 \xrightarrow{t_1} c_1 \xrightarrow{t_2} \cdots \xrightarrow{t_n} c_n = c'$$

Remark. If $n = 0$ above, we simply mean the identity relation.

One could show by straight forward induction that an initial configuration, c_{fact}, with a factorial actor and a task requesting the factorial actor to evaluate the factorial of n possibly goes to a configuration in which a $n!$ communication is sent to the mail address of the customer which was specified in the request to evaluate the factorial of n. When the factorial actor is sent two requests, to evaluate the factorials of the nonnegative integers n_1 and n_2, one can make a stronger statement than the one above: Considering that the computation structure is finite, one can show that there is a set of configurations, C, that c_{fact} necessarily goes to a configuration in C and both the factorial of n_1 and n_2 have been evaluated that configuration. The configurations in C have the interesting property that no further evolution is possible from them without communications being sent by some external actor. We call such a configuration *quiescent* (cf. termination of a computation).

Consider the following example which requires concurrent processing of two requests. Suppose the factorial actor (as we defined it in Examples 3.2.2 and 5.2.1) was sent two communications, one of which was to evaluate the factorial of -1 and the other was to evaluate the factorial of n, where n is some nonnegative integer. The behavior of the factorial actor implies that it would embark on the equivalent of a non-terminating computation. More precisely it would send itself a communication with $-k-1$ in response to a communication with $-k$, and so on, and therefore it cannot possibly evolve to any configuration which is quiescent.

Recall that in the actor model, the delivery of all communications sent is guaranteed. This implies that despite the continual presence of a communication with a negative number in every configuration this configuration possibly goes to, it must at some point process the task with the request to evaluate the factorial of n.[9] We can express this sort of a result by defining the following relation on sets of configurations.

---

[9]This in turn results in the request to evaluate the factorial of $n - 1$. Thus by induction we can establish that at some point in its life, this factorial actor will (indirectly) activate a communication $[n!]$ to the mail address of the customer in the corresponding request.

Definition 5.10 Subsequent Transitions. *A configuration c has a* subsequent transition *to a configuration c' with respect to τ, symbolically* $c \overset{\tau}{\hookrightarrow} c'$ *, if*

$$\tau \in tasks(c) \wedge c \longrightarrow^* c' \wedge \tau \notin tasks(c') \wedge$$
$$\neg \exists c'' (\tau \notin tasks(c'') \wedge c \longrightarrow^+ c'' \wedge c'' \longrightarrow^* c')$$

In simple terms, the subsequent transition represents the first configuration along some computation path which does not contain the task in question. If we defined the set of configurations, X_c^τ, as follows:

$$X_c^\tau = \{c' | c \overset{\tau}{\hookrightarrow} c'\}$$

then the guarantee of mail delivery implies that the configuration c must pass through a configuration in X_c^τ. Subsequent transitions provide a way of defining a fair semantics by derivation for an actor model. The actor model is assumed to have both the possibility transition and the subsequently transitions as primitives. We can define a necessity relation using the subsequent transition. A configuration c *necessarily* goes through a set of configurations X_c, symbolically $c \vartriangleright X_c$, if

$$X_c = \bigcap_{\tau \in T} X_c^\tau$$

where T is the set of tasks in c and X_c^τ is as defined above. X_c represents a set of configurations in which all the tasks of c have been processed. Furthermore, no configurations in X_c can be non-trivially derived from a configuration in which all the tasks of c have been processed. We can extend the necessarily relation to sets by taking the appropriate union. Let C_1 and C_2 be two sets of configurations. C_1 necessarily goes through C_2 if

$$C_2 = \bigcup_{c \in C_1} X_c$$

where $c \vartriangleright X_c$.

The subsequent relation defines what may be considered locally infinite transitions. This is due to the nature of nondeterminism in the actor model. The relation captures the unbounded nondeterminism inherent in the actor paradigm. For a discussion of this phenomenon, see [Clinger 1981]. Some authors have found unbounded nondeterminism to be rather distressing. In particular, it has been claimed that unbounded nondeterminism could never occur in a real system [Dijkstra 1977]. Actually unbounded nondeterminism is ubiquitous due to the quantum physical nature of our universe: it is found in meta-stable states (for a discussion of the implications of meta-stable states for VLSI see [Mead and Conway 1980]).

Chapter 6

Concurrency Issues

In this chapter, we discuss how the actor model deals with some common problems in the theory of concurrent systems. The first section discusses the implications of the actor model for divergence, deadlock, and mutual exclusion. The problem of divergence is severely contained by the guarantee of delivery of communications. In a strict syntactic sense, deadlock cannot occur in an actor system. In a higher level semantic sense of the term, deadlock can occur in a system of actors. Fortunately in the case of a semantic deadlock, the structure of computations in actor systems implies that run-time detection and removal of deadlock is quite feasible.

The second section discusses the relation between dataflow and actors. With respect to functional programming, we show that the concept of side-effect free history sensitive functional computation in *streams* is similar in at least one abstract way to the specification of replacement behavior in actors. In both cases, *history-sensitivity* is achieved by similar functional mechanisms. Finally, we discuss how a sequence of communications from a given sender to a given recipient can be preserved. Although the underlying actor model assumes arrival order nondeterminism, it is certainly possible to define communication channels using actors such that the order of communications between specific actors is preserved.

6.1 Problems in Distributed Computing

There are some problems which are peculiar to distributed systems and cause one to exercise a great deal of caution in exploiting distributed computing. We will discuss three such problems as they relate to actors—namely divergence, deadlock, and mutual exclusion. In each instance, we will show how the actor model provides the mechanisms to allow the programmer to use standard solutions to these problems.

6.1.1 Divergence

A *divergence* corresponds to what is commonly called an "infinite loop." In some cases, such as a process corresponding to a clock or an operating system, an infinitely extending computation is quite reasonable and *termination* may be incorrect (indeed, aggravating!). At the same time, one may want to have the ability to stop a clock in order to reset it, or bring down an operating system gracefully in order to modify it [Hoare 1978]. Thus we would like to program potentially infinite computations that can nevertheless be affected or terminated.

If one looked at the computation tree defined by the possibility transition (see Appendix A) then the execution method of an actor program would seem to be modelled as *choice-point nondeterminism* [Clinger 1981] or *depth search* [Harel 1979]. In this execution scheme, an arbitrary pending communication is nondeterministically accepted by its target causing a transition to the next level in a tree. Using choice-point nondeterminism, it is impossible to guarantee the "termination" of a process which has the potential to extend for an arbitrarily long period of time.

Consider the following simple program. We define the behavior of a stopwatch to be a perpetual loop which can be reset by sending it an appropriate communication (an actor with such a behavior would be useful as a real stopwatch only if we had some additional knowledge about the time it took for the actor to receive and process the "next" communication it sends itself).

$stopwatch(n)$
    if $message = \langle go \rangle$
            then become $stopwatch(n+1)$
                   send $\langle go \rangle$ to *self*
            else become $stopwatch(0)$
                   send $[n]$ to *customer*

Suppose x is created with the behavior $stopwatch(0)$. If x is sent a "go" message, then x will embark on a nonterminating computation. If we wish to "reset" x, we can send it another communication, such as [*customer*, "reset"], where *customer* is the mail address of some actor. If and when this message is processed, x will be "reset." Without the guarantee of delivery of communications, the "reset" message may never be received by x and there would be no mechanism to (gracefully) reset the *stopwatch*. Since the

Figure 6.1: *A finite but unbounded loop. When a* reset *message is processed, one of an infinite number of messages may be sent to the customer because an arbitrary number of* go *messages may have been processed prior to the acceptance of a* reset *message.*

actor model guarantees delivery of communications, x will at some point be "reset." It will subsequently continue to "tick" because it will receive a "go" message sent as a result of the last "go" message processed.

In the case of *stopwatch*, the potentially perpetual activity affects subsequent behavior. This need not always be the case. A "nonterminating" computation can sometimes be "infinite chatter." Indeed, this is the definition of divergence in [Brookes 1983]. We have seen an example of this kind of divergence in the case of our factorial actor when it was sent a message with -1. In a language where the factorial is defined using a looping construct, the factorial could be rendered useless once it accepted a message containing -1. This is because it would embark on a nonterminating computation and therefore never exit the loop in order to accept the next communication. The nontermination of a computation in a language using loops *inside* a process is a serious problem in the context of a distributed system. The process with an infinite loop may be a shared resource—as many processes in a distributed system would be. Since the process is never "done," any other process trying to communicate with it may not do so. This can have a domino effect on the ability of the system to carry out other computations, as more processes end up "waiting" to communicate with processes that are also waiting.

One solution to the problem is to use multiple *activations* of a process. In this framework, each communication to the factorial would activate a process of its own. Activations solve the problem for *unserialized* behavior, as is the case with the factorial. However, when we are interested in a shared object which may actually change its behavior, as is the case with a stopwatch, multiple activations are *not* a solution.

The actor model deals with the problem of divergence whether or not the behavior of actors involved is serialized. Divergence, defined as endless chatter, does not affect other activity in the constructive sense that all pending communications are nevertheless eventually processed. The presence of such divergence simply degrades the *performance* of the system.[1] The guarantee of mail delivery also fruitfully interacts with divergence as the term is used in the broader sense of any (potentially) nonterminating computation.

6.1.2   Deadlock

One of the classic problems in concurrent systems which involve resource sharing is that of *deadlock*. A *deadlock* or *deadly embrace* results in a situation where no further evolution is possible. A classic scenario for a deadlock is as follows. Each process uses a shared resource which it will not yield until another resource it needs is also available. The other resource, however, is similarly locked up by another process. A canonical example of the deadlock problem is the *dining philosophers* problem [Dijkstra 1971]. The problem may be described as follows. Five independent philosophers alternately eat and philosophize. They share a common round table on which each of them has a fixed place. In order to eat, each philosopher requires two chopsticks.[2] A philosopher shares the chopstick to his right with the neighbor to the right and like-wise for the chopstick to his left. It is possible for all the philosophers to enter, pick up their right chopsticks and attempt to pick up the left. In this case, none of the philosophers can eat because there are no free chopsticks.

The behavior of a philosopher and that of a chopstick is described as follows:[3]

$$phil\ (\ left\text{-}chop,\ right\text{-}chop\ )\ [\ ]$$
$$\text{let }x = \text{call }right\text{-}chop\ [\ pick\ ]$$
$$\text{and }y = \text{call }left\text{-}chop\ [\ pick\ ]$$
$$\{\ \text{if }x = \text{free and }y = \text{free then }\langle eat\rangle\ \dots\ \}$$

---

[1] Using resource management techniques, one can terminate computations which continue beyond allocated time. The actor always has a well-defined behavior and would be available for other *transactions* even if some concurrently executing transactions run out of resources.

[2] The usual version is two forks. However, it has never been clear to me why anyone, even a philosopher, would require two forks to eat!

[3] Since we are using expressions, if we were in SAL or *Act*, we would have to specify the behavior in case the reply from the chopstick was not *free*. However, the problem of deadlock has been formulated with no defined behavior in such cases.

Figure 6.2: *The scenario for the Dining Philosophers problem. Five philosophers are seated in a circle and share chopsticks with their neighbor. If each philosopher picks up the chopstick to his right then none of the philosophers can eat. Shared resources can lead to deadlock in sequential processes using synchronous communication.*

```
chopstick (state) [ k ]
    if k = pick and if state = "free"
        then   reply [ free ]
               become chopstick (busy)
    . . .
```

One solution to this problem is to define a *waiter* who acts as a receptionist to the dining area: the waiter can make sure that no more than four philosophers attempt to eat simultaneously. In this case, at least one philosopher will be able to pick up two chopsticks and proceed to eat [Brookes 1983]. This philosopher would subsequently relinquish his chopstick and leave. However, because the waiter may let a new philosopher in as soon as one leaves and fairness is not assumed in synchronous communication models, this solution leaves open the possibility that some philosophers waiting in the dining area in fact starve.

The "waiter solution" is a particular example of the strategy of restricting access to a shared resource in order to avoid the possibility of deadlock. The difficulty with this solution is that mechanisms for avoiding deadlock have to be tailored using advance knowledge about how the system might deadlock. Furthermore, the *waiter* is a bottleneck which may drastically reduce the throughput in a large system. Unfortunately, restricting is the sort of solution used in systems relying on synchronously communicating sequential processes. In a system relying on synchronous communication, the philosopher who picks up his right chopstick cannot communicate with his left chopstick as the left chopstick is "busy" with the philosopher to that chopstick's left. Furthermore, even if a philosopher, $phil_1$, knew that he shared his left chopstick with another philosopher, say $phil_2$, unless $phil_2$ was already ready to communicate with $phil_1$, the latter could not send a message to the former. In such a system, not only is there a deadlock, but there is no mechanism for detecting one. In fact in languages using synchronous communication, deadlock has been defined as a condition where no process is capable of communicating with another [Brookes 1983].

Two areas of Computer Science where the problem of deadlock arises in practice are operating systems and database systems. In operating systems, deadlock avoidance protocols are often used. However, in database systems it has been found that deadlock avoidance is unrealistic [Date 1983]. The reasons why deadlock avoidance is not feasible in concurrent databases can be summarized as follows:

- The set of *lockable objects* (cf. chopsticks in the dining philosophers example) is very large—possibly in the millions.

- The set of lockable objects varies dynamically as new objects are continually created.

- The particular objects needed for a *transaction* (cf. "eating" in our example) must be determined dynamically; i.e., the objects can be known only as the transaction proceeds.

The above considerations are equally applicable to the large-scale concurrency inherent in actor systems. The actor model addresses this problem in two ways. First, no *syntactic* (or low-level) deadlock is possible in an actor system, in the sense of it being impossible to communicate (as in the Brookes' definition above). The chopstick, even when "in use," must designate a replacement and that replacement *can* respond to the philosopher's query. What sort of information is contained in the response, and what the philosopher chooses to do with the reply depends on the program. If each philosopher is programmed to simply keep trying to use the chopstick then in a *semantic* sense the system can indeed be deadlocked. However, notice that one can specify the behavior of the chopstick so that the replacement replies with information about who is using it even while it is "busy." Thus $phil_1$ can query $phil_2$ about $phil_2$'s use of the chopstick shared between them. In the end it would be apparent to the inquisitive philosopher that he was waiting for himself—which is the condition for deadlock.

The most involved aspect of a deadlock is *detecting* it. Because in the actor model every actor must specify a replacement and mail addresses may be communicated, it is possible to detect deadlock. An actor is free and able to figure out a deadlock situation by querying other actors as to their local states. Thus an actor need not be prescient about the behavior of another actor. For example, the ability to communicate mail addresses means that a philosopher need not know in advance which other philosopher or philosophers may be using the chopstick of interest. While these philosophers may be "busy" eating or looking for a chopstick, they nevertheless accept communications sent to them. Thus by requiring that a replacement be specified, a system can continue to evolve.

Our solution is in line with that proposed for concurrent database systems where "wait-for" graphs are constructed and any cycles detected in the graphs are removed [King and Collmeyer 1973]. We would carry out the process of breaking the deadlock in a completely distributed fashion. A concern about deadlock detection is the cost of removing deadlocks. Experience with concurrent databases suggests that deadlocks in large systems occur very infrequently [Gray 1980]. The cost of removing deadlocks is thus likely to be much lower than the cost of any attempt to avoid them.

A system of actors is best thought of as a community of autonomous agents [Hewitt and deJong 1983]. Message-passing viewed in this manner provides a foundation for reasoning in open, evolving systems. Deadlock detection is one particular application of using message-passing for reasoning in an actor system: any actor programmed to be sufficiently clever can figure out why the resource it needs is unavailable and, without remedial action, about to stay that way. To solve this sort of a problem, *negotiation* between independent agents becomes important. In open and evolving systems, new situations will arise and thus the importance of this kind of flexibility is enormous.

Another consequence of reasoning actors is that systems can be easily programmed to "learn": a philosopher may *become* one that has learned to query some particular philosopher who is a frequent user of the chopstick it needs instead of first querying the chopstick. Or the actor may become one which avoids eating at certain times by first querying a clock.

6.1.3 Mutual Exclusion

The *mutual exclusion* problem arises when two processes should never simultaneously access a shared resource. An actor represents *total containment*: it can be "accessed" only by being sent a communication. An actor accepts only a single communication and specifies a replacement which will accept the next communication in its mail queue. The actor may specify a replacement which simply buffers the communications received until the resource is free. We have seen an example of this strategy with *insensitive actors*. Although, a single receptionist may control access to a resource, the resource itself can still be modelled as a system of actors so that there may be concurrency in the use of the resource. When appropriate, there can also be multiple receptionists in a system. In general, a programmer using an actor language need not be concerned with the mutual exclusion problem.

6.2   Streams

In this section we discuss the analogy between the ability to send oneself communications in dataflow and the ability to specify a replacement behavior in actors. We establish the functionality in the behavior of an actor by defining nodes in the spirit of dataflow graphs which illustrate the similarity between the two concepts.

A *stream* is a sequence of values passing through a graph link in the course of a dataflow computation [Weng 1975]. Streams were introduced for 'side-effect free history-sensitive computation.' In this section, we show by analogy to streams that actors are also side-effect free in the same sense of the term. To see the equivalence, consider each node as containing a single behavior definition which is equivalent to all the behavior definitions which may be used by the replacements. The fact that there may be a sequence of definitions in a SAL program is a matter of expressive convenience. Actually, having more than one behavior definition does not really change anything. The identifier used in a new expression is simply a selector of which behavior definition to use and this fact can be communicated just as well. Recall that there are only a finite number of behavior definitions in a program. A single behavior definition which receives an identifier and branches on it to the code corresponding to the behavior would have an equivalent effect. The *become* command in the program is equivalent to sending oneself a communication with the values of acquaintances including the identifier corresponding to the definition to be used in order to determine the replacement behavior.

There is an apparent difference between actors and nodes in dataflow graphs; in dataflow the values "output" form a single stream. So the correspondence can be visualized more closely using the picture Fig. 6.3 which uses appropriate filters on the stream to separate the message intended for the actor itself and that intended for "output."

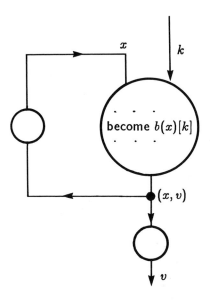

Figure 6.3: *The replacement of an actor can be computed using streams which feed the value of the requisite identifiers for the new behavior. The actor on left separates the values needed for replacement from those needed for "output" while the bottom actor does the converse.*

Of course actors, unlike the elements of dataflow, do more than pass streams—they may change their acquaintances and they may create other actors. Furthermore, actors themselves are not sequential in character and the replacement is concurrently executed. One consequence of this is the ability to use recursive control structures which cannot be used in static dataflow. A variation of the dataflow model allows for fully re-entrant code by tagging the "tokens" (messages) [Gurd, Kirkham and Watson 1985]. Unfortunately, because one cannot dynamically create customers, a tagged token architecture results in forcing the computation through a possible bottleneck instead of distributing it. Although the actor model allows for dynamic creation of actors, the behavior of an actor, like that of a node in a dataflow,[4] is functionally determined.

---

[4]To add to some confusion in the nomenclature, dataflow nodes are referred to as actors in some of the dataflow literature.

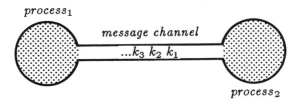

Figure 6.4: *A communication channel preserves the order of communications between two processes. Such channels can be readily defined in actor systems.*

6.3   Message Channels

Many systems preserve the order of messages between processes. A *stream* in some models of dataflow has been defined as a sequence of values—thus by definition it is ordered. This creates the interesting problem in dataflow when the order of input from two sources cannot be predetermined. A special element for nondeterministic *merge* has to be assumed and such an element cannot be defined in terms of the other constructs in the dataflow model.

The preservation of the order of messages between processes is sometimes simply a function of the hardware configuration. For example, in point-to-point communication between two directly connected processors, the message channel preserves the order of communications. Sometimes this property can be usefully exploited in computations. An example of this kind of use is found in [Seitz 1985] which describes a concurrent architecture called the *Cosmic Cube*. The Cosmic Cube is based on 64 processors in a hyper-cube topology. In the current implementation of the cube, multiple processes may reside on a single processor but processes are never migrated. The processes are asynchronous and use message-passing to interact. However, unlike actors the messages are sent along fixed channels so that (coupled with the lack of migration of processes) the order in which messages are sent by a process A to a process B is the same order in which B receives those messages (although other messages may be interleaved).

One can not simply assume a hardware-based preservation of the order of messages. For one, the failure of a single processor would be disastrous since one can not re-route a message and *necessarily* preserve its order in transmission with respect to other messages already sent. For another, this scheme creates difficulties in load balancing since the later requires variable routing of messages and migration of processes. A concurrent architecture can address these issues at some additional cost (see the discussion below). For generality, the actor model assumes nondeterminism in the relation between the order in which communications are sent and the order in which they are received. Such nondeterminism is termed *arrival order nondeterminism.*

It is nevertheless possible to define actors which in effect preserve the order in which they process communications from each other. Suppose we wished that an actor f "processed" communications from an actor g in the same order as they were sent by g. What the actor g needs to do is tag each message it sends to f with a *reference number* and increment that number each time. The actor f in turn remembers the number of messages it has so far processed from g. If it has processed two, and *message number 4* from g arrives next, f simply buffers that communication until it has accepted *message number 3* from g. Since the delivery of communications is guaranteed, the communication enclosing *message number 3* will also arrive. Subsequently, the actor f will check its buffer for *message number 4* and proceed to process the same. The details can be easily written in an actor language. We have shown that it is not necessary to add any new constructs in order to define order-preserving communication channels in an actor language.

The scheme we use to show the definability of channels is similar to that used in Computer Network Architectures where *sequence numbers* are used in *packet switched networks* to carry out sequence checking [Meijer and Peeter 83]. Because doing so introduces extra overhead, we do not make ubiquitous use of virtual network channels.

Chapter 7

Abstraction And Compositionality

The ability to write and debug large software systems is strongly dependent upon how successfully the system can be partitioned into *independent* modules. Modules are independent if we can ignore the details of their internal behavior and treat them as black-boxes with certain input-output behavior. Concurrency involves a nondeterministic interleaving of events; one consequence of such interleaving is that when systems are composed, events in one system are interleaved with the events of the other. Unfortunately, the behavior of the composed system is not necessarily deducible from abstract representations of the behaviors of the modules composed. In this chapter we address these issues as they relate to concurrency in general and our actor language in particular.

7.1   Abstraction

A classic problem in concurrent systems is the difficulty of abstracting away from the operational behavior of a system. Consider a programming language with the assignment command. Let $\mathcal{F}$ be a function which maps commands in the programming language to their respective meanings. Let $S_1 \equiv x := x + 1$ be a command in this language. If n is any given integer, the state $\sigma[\![n/x]\!]$ stands for a state where n is the value of x. Now the meaning of S_1 can be expressed as:

$$\mathcal{F}(S_1): \quad \sigma[\![n/x]\!] \longrightarrow \sigma[\![n + 1/x]\!]$$

Similarly, if $S_2 \equiv x := 2 * x$ then the meaning of S_2 is given by

$$\mathcal{F}(S_2) : \quad \sigma[\![n/x]\!] \quad \longrightarrow \quad \sigma[\![2 * n/x]\!]$$

If we were to compose the commands S_1 and S_2 sequentially, then their meaning functions would also be composed sequentially. However, if we compose the two commands concurrently then the situation is not so simple. Suppose that the command S represents the concurrent composition of S_1 and S_2, i.e., $S \equiv S_1 \parallel S_2$, where $\parallel$ represents concurrent composition. The meaning of S is not obvious: if we started in a state where $x = 2$, then two of the possibilities are that S_1 precedes S_2 or the other way round. In each case, we can deduce the meaning of S by sequentially composing the meanings of S_1 and S_2: after the execution of both commands, x may be 6 or it may be 5. However, it is also possible that the execution overlaps in time. For example, to execute S_1 we may FETCH the value of x, but before S_1 has finished execution, x may be fetched by S_2. In this case, the "final" state could be $\sigma[\![3/x]\!]$ or $\sigma[\![4/x]\!]$, neither of which is obvious from a composition of the denotational meanings of the two commands.[1]

7.1.1   Atomicity

The solution to this problem is usually given by specifying which actions are *atomic*, i.e., by specifying that the execution of certain commands may not be interrupted [deBakker 1980]. For example, if the assignment command is defined to be atomic, then one would need to interleave only the meanings of assignment commands.

The problem with the atomicity solution is that it fixes the level of granularity or detail which must be retained by the meaning function. Thus, if the assignment command is atomic, one must retain information about each and every transformation caused by the execution of an assignment command in a program. This necessarily means that one cannot abstract away the operational details inherent in assignments. If, for example, one is defining the abstract meaning of an iterative loop, all assignments involved in the iterative loop must be retained by the meaning function.

The approach to abstraction in actor systems is somewhat different. The concept of a *receptionist* is defined to limit the interface of a system to the outside. The use of the receptionist concept is illustrated in the context of the assignment example. We define two systems whose behavior differs

---

[1]It may appear that

$$\mathcal{F}(S_1 \parallel S_2) = \mathcal{F}(S_1; S_2) \cup \mathcal{F}(S_2; S_1) \cup \mathcal{F}(S_1) \cup \mathcal{F}(S_2)$$

but one can construct a slightly more complex example where this relation does not hold either.

partly because the receptionist in each is used to attain a different level of abstraction. Consider the first system; x is the receptionist in this system and the behavior of x is as follows:

$x(\,n\,)\;[\langle request \rangle]$
    if $\langle request \rangle$ = FETCH then reply $[\,n\,]$
    if $\langle request \rangle$ = STORE i then become $x(\,i\,)$

The system has the a level of granularity where the behavior of the configuration must be considered in terms of interleaving FETCH and STORE messages. However, in a larger system, x may no longer be a receptionist and it may be possible to avoid this level of detail. For example, let r be the receptionist for an actor system and the behavior of r be given as follows:

$r(n)\;[\langle request \rangle]$
    if $\langle request\ is\ to\ assign\ value\ f(x) \rangle$
        then let $a=f(n)$ { become $r(a)$ }
    if $\langle request\ is\ to\ show\ value \rangle$
        then reply $[\,n\,]$

Note that the nesting of the *become* command inside the let expression creates a sequentiality in the execution (see the discussion about the let construct in Section 4.3). In this larger configuration, one need no longer consider the FETCH or STORE events. The level of granularity is comparable to the atomicity of assignment commands. However, we can define yet larger systems with other receptionists so that these operational details can be ignored as well. We illustrate this concept by means of another example.

7.1.2 Receptionists

Consider a *bank account* which may be accessed through different money machines. Suppose further that this bank account is shared between several users. The behavior for such a bank account may be something like that given in Example 3.3. Now one may want that once an account is accessed through a money machine, it should complete the *transactions* with the user at that machine before accepting requests for transactions from other users. The definition of a bank account as given in Example 3.3 implies that the bank account processes one request at a time but that it may interleave requests from different "users" and "money machines."

To create a system where transactions at each money machine are completed before other transactions are acceptable, we define a larger configuration where the receptionist for the system is some actor called *account-receptionist*. All communications to the account must be sent through this receptionist and the transactions of the account-receptionist consist of several sub-transactions with the users. The behavior of the receptionist may be described as follows:

> *a-free-account*
>> **become** ⟨*a-busy-account with the current customer*⟩
>> ⟨*process the request*⟩
>
> *a-busy-account*
>> **if** *customer* ≠ ⟨*current customer*⟩
>>> **then send** ⟨*request*⟩ **to** *buffer*
>>
>> **if** *customer* = ⟨*current customer*⟩
>>> **then if** ⟨*request = release*⟩
>>>> **then   send** ⟨*release*⟩ **to** *buffer*
>>>> **become** *a-free-account*
>>>
>>> **else** ⟨*process the request*⟩

What the receptionist does is to prevent the interleaving of requests to the account from different users. An analysis of the behavior of this system can thus be done by considering the overall results of transactions from each machine without having to consider all the possible orders in which the requests from different machines may be received. We need to consider the possible order in which entire sets of sub-transactions may occur (since the order in which the first request from a user is received is still indeterminate).

One can construct arbitrarily complex systems so that their behavior is increasingly abstract. There is no predetermined level of "atomicity" for all actor systems. Instead, it is the programmer who determines the degree of abstraction; the concept of receptionists is simply a mechanism to permit greater modularity and hence procedural and data abstraction.

7.2 Composition of Concurrent Systems

One of the desirable features about Milner's *Calculus of Communicating Systems* (CCS) is that it models composition rather effectively. Milner's notion of composition is based on *mutual experimentation* by two machines: a machine S offers experiments which may combine with experiments of another machine T to yield an "interaction." Both machines, as a result

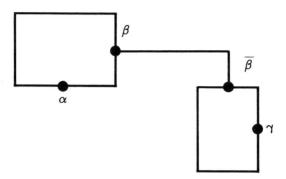

Figure 7.1: *Synchronous composition: In CCS, composition of systems is analogous to plugging machines together. Figure from [Milner 1980].*

of the interaction, change their local states. The concept of interaction is based on intuitions of how machines may be plugged together physically, a notion that relates very well to synchronous communication.

When an interaction between two machines occurs in Milner's system, one simply links the ports on the two machines. Ports that may be linked are considered *complementary ports*. One can *hide* a port provided one also hides its complement. Thus, upon composition, one can abstract away from the ports by an operation called *restriction*.

7.2.1 Actors and Ports

The notion of hiding ports using the restriction operator has somewhat different implications in CCS than its intuitive interpretation seems to be when thinking in terms of actors. When a port and its complement have been restricted, it's the *interaction* between the two that has been hidden. As a result of the interaction, the port will subsequently unfold its behavior and this behavior will <u>not</u> be hidden. Thus, to use actor jargon, the port may "become" another port which may even have the same label as the one that is hidden. In terms of actors, the restriction operator is equivalent to hiding the acceptance of a *single* communication; it is <u>not</u> equivalent to hiding all the communications which may be received by a given actor.

A system of actors is best thought of as a *community of agents*. The agents retain their identity even as their behavior changes. Actors have mail addresses which permanently identify them. The *behavior objects* in

CCS do not necessarily maintain any "identity" as they interact with the other objects. For example, in CCS once an agent accepts an input, it may never accept another input on the same port because, as a result of processing the communication, it *may* no longer even have the same port. Besides the ports do not uniquely identify an agent: different agents may use the same port name and, as a consequence, different complementary ports may be linked. In contrast, communications in actors are sent to a specific unique target actor.

There are other differences between the behavior of an agent in CCS and that of an actor. One of these is that agents in CCS are themselves sequential in character: only *one* experiment may be performed at a time. The justifications Milner provides for this sequentiality are:

1. Tractability of the model; and,

2. The desire to have a behavior object represent the system according to an observer capable of only one experiment at a time.

We gave a similar argument about the import of using nondeterminism to model concurrency (Section 5.2). The fact remains that concurrency includes the potential for overlap in time in both models. There is, however, a fundamental difference between Milner's "behavior objects" and the behavior of an actor: the actor itself is a concurrent agent. The difference is reflected in the language defined by Milner to illustrate CCS and actor languages: in the former, sequentiality is intrinsic; in the latter, it is present only due to causal interactions (Section 4.3).

7.2.2   Encapsulation in Actors

Any system must have receptionists which can accept information from the "outside," and any system must know of agents that are external to the system. The designation of receptionists and external actors provides for structuring the input-output behavior (or, what in other fields would be called the stimulus-response or sensori-motor aspects) of a system. There are several observations to be made here which are relevant to actor systems:

- An actor which serves as a receptionist may also be known to other actors within the system. Communications between such *internal* actors and a receptionist will not be observable. Thus it is not so much an actor that is visible or hidden, but rather it is communications between a given *sender-target* pair that are observable when either the sender or the target is external. (See Fig. 7.2.)

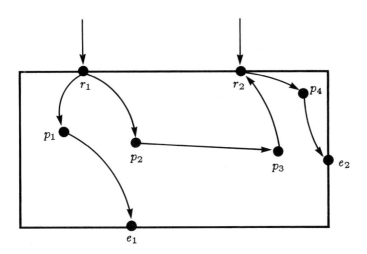

Figure 7.2: *Communications sent by p_3 to r_2 are not observable in an encapsulated system, just as those sent by r_1 to p_1 are internal.*

- As a system evolves, *new receptionists* may be added and *new external actors* may become known. The mechanism for this change is simply the ability to send messages containing mail addresses.

- One can <u>not</u> arbitrarily restrict receptionists: once a mail address has been communicated to the outside, it is available for use by external actors. However, if a mail address is unknown to the outside, or becomes unknown, then the actor is no longer a receptionist.

7.2.3 Composition Using Message-Passing

Composition in actors is achieved by message-passing. Independent systems are connected by sending some buffers for external actors in each module a communication to become *forwarding* actors which simply send their mail to some receptionists in the other module. The justification for the term "become" in the specification of replacement actors is the same as the reason why the external actors and receptionists they forward their mail to are equivalent in a message-passing semantics. We observe the following:

Proposition: *If the behavior of an actor x is unserialized, and its behavior*

*is to forward all the communications it accepts to an actor y, then sending
a communication to x is equivalent to sending the communication to y.*

The proposition is a consequence of the arrival order nondeterminism
in the actor model. A communication sent to the actor x will be eventually
received by the actor y. Since the arrival of a communication is always subject to an arbitrary delay, even if the communication was originally targeted
to y, it would have arrived at some indeterminate time at y. Note that the
guarantee of mail delivery is essential in establishing this proposition because otherwise it would be possible for x to receive a communication and
yet for y to never receive the same.

Given a configuration with a forwarding actor, we can construct an
equivalent configuration without the forwarding actor by replacing the forwarding actor's mail address in the acquaintance lists of all actors and
tasks in the configuration defined with the mail address of the actor to
which it forwards the communications it receives. The two configurations
can be said to be equivalent in some semantic sense. When an actor x acquires the unserialized behavior to forward all communications it receives
to an actor y, the actor x is said to become a *forwarder* to y. Using the
above proposition as justification we will assume that two such actors are
equivalent.

The rules to compose configurations are developed and these may be
used to compose systems by composing configurations they may be in.
All composition will be done using message-passing, and as a consequence
there is no need to assume uniqueness in the configuration at the "time"
of composition of a system: the exact evolution of the composed system
is nondeterministic because of the nondeterminism in the arrival order of
the communications. In actor systems, because there is an arbitrarily long
delay in the delivery of messages, no special construction is necessary to
represent the composition of two systems.

7.2.4   Rules for Composition

In this section we develop the constraints that must be satisfied by any
scheme which carries out the composition of two systems. We provide
the constraints in terms of configurations and assert their realizability by
showing a definition of composition which would satisfy the conditions. To
compose actor programs, one would map them to the initial configurations
they define and compose these configurations using the rules of composition
given.

Constraints on Interface Actors

We first define all the applicable rules for constraining the actors that interface with the outside—i.e., the set of receptionists and external actors for a composed system.

Let $extern(c_1)$ represent the actors which are external to a configuration c_1, and $recep(c_2)$ represent actors which serve as receptionists in a configuration c_2, then there may be some actor x such that $x \in extern(c_1) \cap recep(c_2)$. It is also possible (but <u>not</u> necessary) that when c_1 and c_2 are composed, such an actor x is no longer a receptionist of the composed system because the only actors x may have been a receptionist for are in the other system composed. In any case, x will <u>not</u> be external to the composed system. Let $c \equiv c_1 \parallel c_2$, where $\parallel$ represents the composition operator. We can assert the following properties about the receptionists and external actors of c:

1. All receptionists in the composed system must be receptionists in one of the two configurations:

$$recep(c) \subset recep(c_1) \cup recep(c_2)$$

2. The only actors which may no longer be the receptionists are actors that are external to one of the configurations composed:

$$(recep(c_1) \cup recep(c_2)) - recep(c) \subset extern(c_1) \cup extern(c_2)$$

3. All external actors in a composed configuration must be external to one of the two configurations:

$$extern(c) \subset extern(c_1) \cup extern(c_2)$$

4. The only actors which may no longer be external are actors that are receptionists for one of the configurations composed:

$$(extern(c_1) \cup extern(c_2)) - extern(c) \subset recep(c_1) \cup recep(c_2)$$

Since we want the identifiers in an actor program (and correspondingly the mail addresses in a configuration) to be local to the module (or to the configuration), we have to provide a means of "relabeling" identifiers so as to link receptionists and external actors. Thus when two program modules are composed, we may have a declaration of the form:

$$\mathsf{let}\ \ id_1 = id_2\ \ \mathsf{and}\ \ id_3 = id_4\ \ \ldots$$

where id_1 is the identifier for an external actor in the first module, and id_2 is an identifier for a receptionist in the second, or vice-versa. Similarly for id_3 and id_4, and so on. The intended interpretation of the above declaration is that in order to compose two modules, we simply send an appropriate communication to the external actors in each of the modules telling them which receptionist in the other module they should become a forwarding actor to.

One cannot necessarily deduce the receptionists of a composed system from the receptionists of its constituents: some receptionists may have been so designated only because they were supposed to represent *external* actors in the 'other' module. Thus a new receptionist declaration may be given for a composed system, provided that such a declaration satisfies the first two properties given above.

Formalizing Composition

We now turn to developing a detailed definition for composing two configurations. To be precise, assume a configuration is a four tuple with the functions *states*, *tasks*, *recep*, and *extern* extracting each component. (We are expanding the definition of a configuration used in Chapter 5 which was concerned more specifically with the internal evolution of an actor system and thus took into account only the first two components.) The *population* of a configuration c, $pop(c)$, consists of mail addresses that are in c but are not elements of $extern(c)$. Suppose c_1 and c_2 are two configurations. To compose c_1 and c_2, we need to specify the new receptionists and external actors. Notice that if c_1 and c_2 are arbitrary configurations and we assume that mail addresses are local to a configuration (recall that mail addresses are merely ways of labeling actors to specify topological properties of a system), then there is no guarantee that $pop(c_1) \cap pop(c_2) = \emptyset$. Similarly, if $tags(c)$ is the set of tags used in the $tasks(c)$, then it is possible that $tags(c_1) \cap tags(c_2) \neq \emptyset$.

In fact, even if the populations and tags of two configurations are disjoint, the *states* and the *tasks* cannot be simply combined using the union operation. To see why, recall the prefix condition in the definition of a configuration (Definition 5.3) and its use in Theorem 5.1: The condition states that no tag be the prefix of any other tag or mail address in a configuration. This property is necessary to maintain the uniqueness of all tags and mail addresses of tasks created.

Tags and mail addresses have no reality of their own. They are merely labels we define to keep track of computation in an actor system. So we will provide a map to new tags and mail addresses in a composed system so that the new tags maintain the structure implied by the original tags and at the same time satisfy the requisite constraints. Providing a map to carry out the composition has no intrinsic value but simply demonstrates the ability to carry out composition.

Definition 7.1 Composition. *Suppose that c, c_1 and c_2 are configurations such that $c = c_1 \parallel_{D,R} c_2$, where D is a declaration equating external actors and receptionists, and R is a receptionist declaration satisfying the constraints given above. Let the declarations in D be equivalences of the form i.e $\approx$ j.r where $i,j \in \{1,2\}$, $e \in extern(c_i)$ and $r \in recep(c_j)$. Then the following conditions hold:*

1. *The tags and mail addresses are simply prefixed by the configuration they came from. Thus,*

$$tasks(c) = \{(i.t, i.m, k') \mid (t, m, k) \in tasks(c_i) \wedge k' = k[\![i.t/t, \ldots]\!]\}$$

2. *The states of all actors not in the declaration D are unchanged except for the transformation on the mail addresses. Let $\underline{forwarder}(x)$ represent the behavior of an actor which sends all communications it accepts or has buffered on to x, then*

$$states(c)(i.m) = \begin{cases} \underline{forwarder}(j.r) & if\ i.m \approx j.r\ in\ D \\ b & otherwise\ given\ (m, b) \in c_i \end{cases}$$

3. *The external actors are those who have not been declared to be equivalent to some receptionist in the composed system.*

$$extern(c) = (\chi_1(c_1) - \{x \mid \exists r \in recep(c_2)(x \equiv 2.r \in D)\}) \cup (\chi_2(c_2) - \{x \mid \exists r \in recep(c_1)(x \equiv 1.r \in D)\})$$

where $\chi_i(c_i) = \{i.x \mid x \in extern(c_i)\}$

4. *The receptionists of c are given by the declaration R.*

Note that our definition can be easily extended to composition of an arbitrary number of configurations. Concurrent composition should of course be commutative and associative. In our definition, the configurations themselves would be different depending on the order of composition. However, there is a strong equivalence relation between the resulting configurations, namely a *direct relabeling* equivalence. Since there are only a finite number of tags and mail addresses the problem of determining the direct relabeling equivalence of any two configurations is decidable.

To compose already existing systems, we need to compose all the configurations the systems may be in. Let $c_1 + c_2$ represent the fact that a system may be in configuration c_1 or in configuration c_2 then:

$$(c_1 + c_2) \parallel (c_3 + c_4) = (c_1 \parallel c_3) + (c_1 \parallel c_4) + (c_2 \parallel c_3) + (c_2 \parallel c_4)$$

where any declarations in the composition on the left hand side of the equation are carried out to each of the terms in the right hand side.

7.3   The Brock-Ackerman Anomaly

An algebra of concurrent processes is defined over equivalence classes of the processes.[2] The *canonical members* of each equivalence class provide an abstract representation for all the processes in the class. There are two considerations in defining equivalence relations. On the one hand, the abstract representation of processes must discriminate between systems which when operated on or composed with other systems lead to behaviors we wish to distinguish from each other. On the other hand, the representation must not discriminate between systems that behave identically in all *contexts*. A context is determined by the degree of encapsulation and the "environment" of other processes it interacts with.

In the case of sequential programs, a *history relation* which maps inputs to outputs is sufficient to provide an abstract characterization of a program. Note that this history relation is distinct from the *history ordering* imposed on actor event diagrams discussed in Section 3.1. Actor event diagrams represent a record of all events in system; they do not hide any information about the system. Representing actor programs in terms of the history order on actor event diagrams does not provide sufficient abstraction; the equivalence relation induced differentiates between too many similarly behaving programs. In this section, we will use the term *history relation* to refer to the relation between inputs and outputs. Note that in the context of actor systems, input refers to communications from an actor outside the configuration to a receptionist, and output to communications from an actor inside the configuration to an external actor.

In the context of concurrent systems, a history relation between inputs and outputs is one of the weakest equivalence relations which may be used to model systems. In other words, it contains the *minimal* information necessary to differentiate between systems. Unfortunately, as [Keller 1977] and [Brock and Ackerman 1981] have shown, the history relation is not sufficient to discriminate between systems that are observably different. Of the two cases cited, the Brock-Ackerman anomaly represents a more serious problem. We discuss it in the context of actor systems.

The Brock-Ackerman anomaly shows that when each of two systems with the same history relations is composed with an identical system, the two resulting combined systems have distinct history relations. Let $\mathcal{H}$ be a

---

[2]In this section we use the term process to impart a general flavor to the discussion. In particular, systems of actors are "processes."

function mapping a process to the history relation it defines. We convert the relation into a function by using the standard technique of collecting all the terms representing the possible elements which are related to each given element of the domain. We first define two actor systems S_1 and S_2 such that they induce identical history relations $\mathcal{H}(S_1) = \mathcal{H}(S_2)$. We then define a system U and show that $\mathcal{H}(S_1 \parallel U) \neq \mathcal{H}(S_2 \parallel U)$ where $\parallel$ represents a concurrent composition.

The receptionist in both systems S_1 and S_2 is an actor whose behavior is described by:

$D(a)$ $[k]$
    send $[k]$ to a
    send $[k]$ to a

In other words D accepts a communication and sends two copies of it to an acquaintance a. The behavior of D is unserialized. The external actor in both systems S_1 and S_2 is called *extern-acq*. In S_1 the behavior of the acquaintance a is to retain the first communication it accepts and to send it and the second communication accepted to *extern-acq*. It can be described as:

$P_1(\textit{inputs-so-far, external-acq, first-input})$ $[k]$
    if *inputs-so-far=0* then become $P_1(1, \textit{external-acq}, k)$
    if *inputs-so-far=1* then
        become SINK
        send $[\textit{first-input}]$ to *external-acq*
        send $[k]$ to *external-acq*

where the behavior of a SINK is simply to "burn" all communications it accepts.

Now a system whose population is $\{d, p_1\}$, with behaviors $D(p_1)$ and $P_1(0, e, 0)$, respectively, and whose external actor is e, has the history relation which maps:

$$\emptyset \;\rightarrow\; \emptyset$$
$$\{x_1\} \;\rightarrow\; \{y_1\ y_1\}$$
$$\{x_1\ x_2\} \;\rightarrow\; \{y_1\ y_1\ ,\ y_1\ y_2\ ,\ y_2\ y_2\}$$

where x_i is the communication k_i sent to the target d, and y_i is the communication k_i sent to the target e. Recall the arrival order nondeterminism in actors; thus sending x_1 followed by x_2, i.e. $x_1\ x_2$, is the same as sending x_2 followed by x_1 since the communications may arrive in any order at the target d, regardless of the order in which they are sent. Internally, when d accepts $[k_1]$ it will send two k_1 messages to p_1 and similarly for k_2. However, these four communications to p_1 may be interleaved in an arbitrary manner. In general the history relation induced by this system can be represented as:

$$x_1 \ldots x_n \rightarrow \{y_i \, y_j \mid 1 \le i, j \le n\}$$

Now consider an actor system S_2 with a receptionist d which has an acquaintance p_2. The initial behavior of p_2 is described by $P_2(0, e)$ where:

> $P_2(\textit{inputs-so-far, external-acq}) \; [k]$
>   send $[\,k\,]$ to *external-acq*
>   if *inputs-so-far*$=0$ then become $P_1(1, \textit{external-acq})$
>   if *inputs-so-far*$=1$ then become SINK

The difference between the (initial) behavior of p_1 and p_2 is that p_1 waits for two inputs before forwarding them both whereas p_2 forwards two inputs as they are received. However, one can readily observe that because of arrival order nondeterminism the history relation on the system S_2 is identical to that on system S_1.

Suppose that each of the actor systems S_i are composed with another actor system U where r_U is the receptionist and has the (unserialized) behavior $E(e_1, e_2)$, where E is as follows:

> $E(\textit{external-acq1} , \textit{external-acq2}) \; [k]$
>   send $[k]$ to *external-acq2*
>   send $[k]$ to *external-acq1*
>   send $[5 * k]$ to *external-acq1*

In U both e_1 and e_2 are external. When we compose S_i with U, d is the only receptionist and e_2 the only external actor in the composed system. The external actor e_1 in U is declared to be the receptionist d (see fig 7.3). The history relation on T_1 which is the composition of S_1 and U maps

$$x_1 \rightarrow y_1 \, y_1$$

where y_1 is the message k_1 to e_2. Note that p_1 has accepted both communications *before* forwarding them to e_2. However, the history relation on T_2 maps

$$x_1 \rightarrow \{y_1 \, y_1 \, , \, y_1 \, y_1'\}$$

where y_1' is the message $5 * k_1$ sent to e_2. This happens because the second k_1 sent to p_2 may arrive *after* the $5 * k_1$ message sent by e_1 has been forwarded and accepted by p_1.

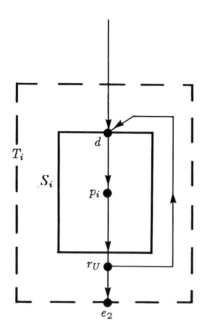

Figure 7.3: *The Brock-Ackerman anomaly. When the systems S_1 and S_2 are composed with a system U which has the population r_U, the history relations of the two composed systems are quite different.*

The Brock-Ackerman anomaly demonstrates the insufficiency of the history relation in representing the behavior of actor systems (in fact, in any processes which have a nondeterministic merge in them). The problem with the history relation is that it ignores the open, interactive nature of systems which may accept communications from the outside and send communications out at any stage. Having sent a communication, the system is in a different set of possible configurations than it was before it did so, and provided we have a model for the behavior of a system, we can deduce that the number of possible configurations it may be in has been reduced. Thus the two systems, S_1 and S_2 are different to begin with because after having sent a communication to the outside, their response to subsequent communications from the outside is distinct.

7.4   Observation Equivalence

We have seen two equivalence relations on configurations in the previous sections. The first of these was a *direct relabeling* equivalence and the second was the equivalence induced by a *history relation*. Neither of these equivalences is satisfactory. The history relation was shown to be too weak: it collapses too many configurations into the same equivalence class.

The equivalence relation induced by direct relabeling is not satisfactory in an admittedly direct sense. For example, suppose two configurations were identical except that at one mail address m the actors in their respective *states* differed in that only the tags and mail addresses created by them were unequal. (This could happen using our definition of the behavior function if, for example, the order of new expressions was different). Using direct equivalence, these configurations would not be mapped to the same equivalence class. What we would like to do is to consider configurations that have transitions to equivalent configurations equivalent. Fortunately an inductive definition, establishing equivalence to depth n for an arbitrary depth, is not necessary for this purpose: Since there are only a finite number of behavior definitions, their equivalence under relabeling can be directly established as well.

Unfortunately, this weaker relabeling equivalence is not satisfactory either. Consider two configurations which are identical *except* that one of them has an actor x such that:

1. x is <u>not</u> a receptionist;

2. x is <u>not</u> the target of any task in the configuration; and

3. the mail address of x is <u>not</u> known to any other actor and is <u>not</u> in any of the communications pending in the configuration.

It can be safely asserted that the two configurations, with and without the actor x, are equivalent (see Section 3.1.1). In implementation terms, the actor x would be a suitable candidate for *garbage collection*. In a semantic sense, there is no observable difference between the two systems. However, these two configurations are clearly not equivalent under relabeling.

We therefore need to define a notion of *observation equivalence* between configurations (following [Milner 1980]). The only events "observable" in an encapsulated system are of two kinds:

- Communications sent from the outside to some receptionist; and

- Communications sent by an actor in the population to an external actor.

This suggests three kinds of transitions from each configuration: transitions involving the acceptance of a communication sent from the outside to a receptionist (input), transitions involving the sending of a communication to an external actor (output), and internal actions (corresponding to processing a task in the configuration which is internal to the configuration). The first kind of transition leads to a configuration c' from a given configuration c such that $tasks(c') = tasks(c) \cup \tau$ where τ is the task accepted from the outside. The other two kinds transitions are the ones already defined in Chapter 5, except that we ignore the labels on all transitions that are not targeted to an external actor. We can now identify computation in actor systems as a tree with these three kinds of labels on its branches (see Appendix A).

How does the composition of trees work in this framework? In CCS, when two trees are combined, the inputs and outputs are matched; the interpretation is that a synchronous communication has occurred. The communication can be masked and the combined transition is called a *silent transition*. Rather surprisingly, no change in the technical aspect of this definition is necessary to accommodate composition in actor systems despite the fact that communication is *asynchronous* in actor systems. The reason is simply as follows: only the acceptance of a communication constitutes a transition from a configuration; thus when two configurations are composed all we are doing is *reconciling* the acceptance of a communication by an external actor with the subsequent behavior of that actor. The latter is given by the actions in the tree corresponding to the configuration where the actor is a receptionist. Because of arrival order nondeterminism, the arrival of the communication is delayed arbitrarily long in the first configuration; thus the composition is, in effect, asynchronous.

A configuration can be extensionally defined using the tree of events specified above. The definition is inductive—two configurations are observation equivalent to degree n if they have have the same observable transitions at the $n\underline{th}$ level of the tree. This notion differentiates between all the configurations one would want to differentiate between. The intuition here is that if it is impossible to observe the difference between two configurations despite any interaction one may have with the systems involved, then there is no point discriminating between the two systems.

Brock has proposed a model of dataflow in terms of *scenarios* which relate the inputs and the outputs of a system using a causal order between them [Brock 1983]. The model however has several limitations, such as fixed input and output "ports," and it does not support compositionality. The first of these two deficiencies is related to the lack of a labeling scheme such as is afforded by the mail address abstraction in actors. Because input and output ports in dataflow are static, this limitation of the scenarios model is not of consequence to dataflow.

One view of causality is that it is nothing more than necessary sequentiality: after all, the pragmatic significance of imputed causal inference in the physical world is simply an expectation of sequentiality in the spatiotemporal order between events considered to be the cause and those considered to be the effect. The inference of all causal relations is an open-ended, undecidable problem since the observation of a cause may be separated from the observation of an effect by an arbitrary number of events. The same *arbitrary delay property* is true of the guarantee of mail delivery. Both of these properties may only be deduced from a proposed model of the internal workings of a system rather than from observations on a system. In contradistinction, the notion of observation equivalence is based on the testability of equivalence to an arbitrary depth.[3]

The problem with the history relation is that it ignores the open, interactive nature of systems. A system may accept a communication at any time, and given that it has produced a particular communication, its response to a subsequent input may be different because of the transitions it has undergone to produce that particular communication. The communication produced is of course simply symptomatic of the change in the system. Internally the change has already occurred, whether or not we have observed its external manifestation—i.e., whether or not the communication sent has been received. On the one hand, until we observe the effects of the change, from an external perspective it is uncertain as to whether the change has already occurred. On the other hand, after we have observed the effects of a transition, we have at best a model for how the system was at the time the transition occurred rather than a model of its "current" status.[4] However, if we have some understanding of the mechanics of a system and we are given a communication from the system, we can prune the tree of possible transitions that the system may have taken.

---

[3]Admittedly, a curious proposition since we can test only one path of possible evolutions of a system. The usual solution to this difficulty is having an arbitrary number of systems predetermined to be equivalent, presumably in some stronger physical sense. The idea is to experiment on these systems in different ways to determine their behavior to any desired degree.

[4]Compare the reasoning behind the old *Heisenberg Uncertainty Principle* to the situation here. An interesting discussion of "quantum physics and the computational metaphor" can be found in [Manthey and Moret 1983].

Chapter 8

Conclusions

We have developed a foundational model of concurrency. The model uses very few primitive constructs but nevertheless satisfies the requirements for a general model of concurrent computation in distributed systems. it differs from models of concurrency based on sequential processes primarily in two respects: it does <u>not</u> assume synchronous communication, and it explicitly provides for the dynamic creation of new mail addresses. The of transition system in actors provides a kind of pure calculus for concurrency.

Actors integrate useful features of functional programming and object-oriented programming. While other functional systems have some measure of difficulty dealing with history-sensitive shared objects, actors can model such objects quite easily. At the same time, actors avoid sequential bottlenecks caused by assignments to a store. In the context of parallel processing, the concept of a store has been the nemesis of the von Neumann architecture.

Actors are inherently parallel and exploit maximal concurrency by dynamically creating customers and by pipelining the replacement process. The creation of customers allows a computation to be distributed between independent agents. The semantics of replacement is fundamentally different from changes to a local store: replacements may exist concurrently. This kind of pipelining can be a powerful tool in the exploitation of parallel processors. Pipelining has already been an extremely successful tool in speeding up computation on many processors currently in use. Unfortunately, the degree to which pipelining can be carried out in the current generation of processors is restricted by ubiquitous assignments to a store, and by the use of global states implicit in a program counter. Actors allow pipelining to be carried out to its logical limits—constrained only by the structure of the computation and by the hardware resources available.

Perhaps the most attractive feature of actor languages is that programmers are liberated from explicitly coding details such as when and where to force parallelism; they can instead concentrate on thinking about the parallel complexity of the algorithm used. If one is to exploit massive parallelism, concurrently using hundreds (and eventually, perhaps millions) of processors, it is not feasible to require programmers of concurrent systems to explicitly create every process that is to be concurrently executed. It is our conjecture that actors will provide a suitable means for exploiting parallelism that has been made feasible by the advent of distributed systems based on VLSI technology.

Message-passing is elemental to computation in actors. The time complexity of communication thus becomes the dominant factor in program execution. More time is likely to be spent on communication lags than on primitive transformations of the data. Architectural considerations such as load balancing, locality of reference, process migration, and so forth, acquire a pivotal role in the efficient implementation of actor languages.

The information provided by a transitional model of actor systems is too detailed to be of "practical" use. The structure of transactions and transaction-based reasoning for the verification of actor programs needs to be studied. The semantics developed here will simply provide a justification for such axiomatic treatment. The open and interactive nature of actors implies that any description of actor behavior will necessarily involve a combinatorial explosion in the exact configurations possible in a system. However, by establishing invariants in the behavior of an actor system, we can satisfy ourselves as to its correctness. The importance of proving program correctness in concurrent systems is underscored by the fact that it is not possible to adequately test such systems in practice. In particular, arrival order nondeterminism implies that any particular sequence of message delivery need never be repeated regardless of the number of tests carried out.

Another critical problem for computer architectures that support actors is to control computational activity. Because actors may be shared objects, one cannot simply assign them, upon their creation, a fixed amount of computational resource. If transactions involving the same actors are concurrently executed, the resources used by each transaction need to be assessed separately. Furthermore, since many messages may be sent in response to a single message, concurrent sub-transactions are spawned dynamically in actor systems. These sub-transactions must also be allocated resources dynamically. Since it is impossible to correctly predict the computational resources needed for a given transaction, allocations have to be continually monitored. In general, the problem of resource allocation is intractable if transactions are not properly nested.

We have addressed a number of general problems that plague computation in distributed systems. Among these problems are deadlock, divergence, abstraction, and compositionality. The problem of deadlock is dealt with by the universal replacement requirement. The effects of divergence on the semantics of a computation are contained by the guarantee of mail delivery. The problem of abstraction is addressed by the concepts of receptionists and transactions and, at the model-theoretic level, by the notion of observation equivalence. And finally, we support composition using pure message-passing.

Future work in actors will provide a concurrent architecture which exploits fine-grained concurrency and is suitable for Artificial Intelligence applications. There are two distinct areas in which research has to proceed. First, a new kind of network architecture is needed. The network architecture must be based on message-driven chip and must provide a mail system with extremely low latency in communication time. A message-driven processor would have a small memory and would carry out the primitive actor instructions in hardware. The architecture itself would be hierarchically designed; the mail system and the distributed operating system are themselves systems of actors which have been realized in the hardware.

The second area in which further research needs to be done is in the development of appropriate linguistic support for description and reasoning methods. Conceptual organization of knowledge is provided by description systems which support inheritance. Descriptions can often be organized along a lattice of specializations and generalizations; such lattices provide a way of storing information efficiently and reasoning about it. Implementing descriptions in actors allows the integration of procedural and declarative information into the same nodes; it also allows description hierarchies to be dynamically reconfigurable. Thus an actor-based description system is capable of re-organizing itself as a result of interaction with its environment. Future research in these areas will likely yield a new generation of actor-based computers whose capabilities far exceed those of the current generation.

Appendix A

Asynchronous Communication Trees

Milner has developed an elegant calculus for synchronously communicating agents (called CCS) [Milner 1980]. As an aid to visualizing computation in a system of such agents, Milner has proposed *Communication Trees* (CTs) as a model for CCS. As Milner has observed, CTs are actually more powerful than CCS; in other words, there are large classes of CTs which cannot be expressed as programs in CCS. For example, the topology implied by CCS is static whereas there is no such restriction on CTs. We develop *Asynchronous Communication Trees* (Υ's) as a model to aid in visualizing computation in actors and a means by which we can define composition, direct equivalence, observation equivalence, etc., in actor systems. The intriguing feature of Υ's is that they capture the open, interactive nature of computation in actors. It is recommended that the reader carefully study Milner's work, in particular Chapters 5 and 6 of [Milner 1980], before trying to work out the material here in any depth.

There are three fundamental differences between actors and CCS:

- Communication is *synchronous* in CCS while it is *asynchronous* in actors.

- The topology on CCS agents is static while communications in actors may contain mail addresses.

- There is no dynamic creation of new labels for ports in CCS while new actors have distinct new mail addresses which are computed dynamically.

Rather surprisingly, the algebra used to define Υ's is almost identical to that used in CTs; the primary difference is in the concrete interpretations associated with each. We interpret only the *acceptance* of a communication as a transition (what Milner calls "action"): Sending a communication is simply represented by the fact that *every* branch of the tree has a transition corresponding to the acceptance of the communication by its target. This fact follows from the guarantee of mail delivery.

We represent each configuration as an Υ. A few simplifying assumptions will be made. First, we assume that there are no mail address conflicts between different configurations (since we provide a relabeling operator, this is without loss of generality). Second, we assume that the external mail addresses represent the true mail address of the external actor. This will be a useful simplification when two configurations are composed. The justification for this assumption is two-fold: first, using message-passing the external actor *forwards* all mail it has received to the actor it is supposed to become; and second, the communications it sent to the external actor can arrive in any order. Third, we assume that there are a countable number of communications, which may be enumerated as $k_0, k_1, \ldots$. Any communication may be sent to any actor, if the communication sent is inappropriate (such as having the wrong number of "parameters"), then we assume there is a default behavior. We can further assume that the tags of tasks are part of the enumeration of communications and used to create new mail addresses.[1] However, tagging tasks is not useful in defining observation equivalence; furthermore, it is also possible to specify a different mechanism to create mail addresses using other mail addresses. The technical development here remains quite similar to CCS.

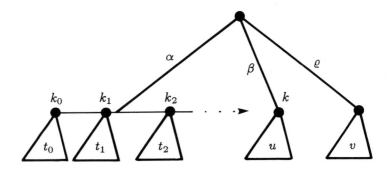

Figure A.1: *A typical Asynchronous Communication Tree*

---

[1] Recall that a union of all finite collections of a countable set is still countable.

A typical Υ consists looks like Fig A.1. The three kinds of *potential transitions* (or in Milner's terminology, *actions*) have the following intuition:

(i) Corresponding to each current receptionist in the configuration is a *potential transition* labeled by its mail address (these are the positive labels, $\alpha, \ldots$, in the figure) and the communication the receptionist may accept. The $i\underline{th}$ tree it dominates represents the behavior of the configuration if the receptionist accepts a communication k_i. An incoming communication may add new external actors.

(ii) For all communications accepted by an external actor, there is a transition to a tree corresponding to the behavior of a configuration without the pending communication. These transitions are labeled by the mail address of the external actor (using negative labels $\overline{\alpha}, \ldots,$). An outgoing communication may add receptionists.

(iii) For all communications accepted by an actor in the population, there is an *internal transition* (labeled by ϱ).[2]

The relation between configurations and Υ's should be intuitively clear from the above description. If each node were marked by the configuration it represented, then (i) would correspond to a transition from a configuration c to a configuration c' such that $states(c) = states(c')$ and $tasks(c') = tasks(c) \cup \tau$ where τ is the task received from the outside; (ii) is the acceptance of a communication by an external actor, and (iii) is acceptance of a communication by any actor in the population.

When an actor accepts a communication, it may create other actors or send new communications to specific targets. These will simply show up in the subsequent behavior of the configuration to which the transition is made. We do not label nodes in our trees (cf. Milner's CTs) because the label would be simply another way of noting the sub-tree dominated by the given node. Formally we define an Υs as follows:

Definition A.1 Asynchronous Communication Trees. *Assume the function $acq(k)$ represents the actors communicated in k. An asynchronous communication tree with receptionists R and external actors E is a finite set[3] of pairs of the form*

---

[2]Milner represents internal transitions, or what he terms "silent actions," by τ but we used that letter to denote tasks.

[3]We do not need a multiset because all mail addresses are unique. However, asynchronous communication trees in their full generality may lack rules guaranteeing uniqueness of mail addresses. Technically this does not create any difficulty; it simply changes the nature of nondeterminism.

(i) $< \alpha, f >$ where $\alpha \in R$ and f is a family of Υ's with receptionists R and external actors $E \cup acq(k_i)$ indexed by possible communications k_i accepted; or,

(ii) $< \overline{\beta}, < k, t >>$ where $\overline{\beta} \in E$, k is a communication targeted to the mail address β and t is an Υ with receptionists $R \cup acq(k)$ and external actors E; or,

(iii) $< \varrho, t >$ where ϱ is an internal transition and t is an Υ with receptionists R and external actors E.

Remark.   We will now define an algebra of Υ's and then define three operations namely, *composition*, *restriction*, and *relabeling* on the Υ's. The actual algebra is almost identical to CTs, with differences in the notion of receptionists and external actors. CTs used sorts which were a fixed set for each CT. The concrete interpretations placed on the terms are, of course, quite different. The definitions below are adapted from [Milner 1980].

Let $\Upsilon_{R \times E}$ denote the Υ's with receptionists R and external actors E and $k_0, k_1, \ldots$, denote the possible communications. We have an algebra of Υ's as follows:

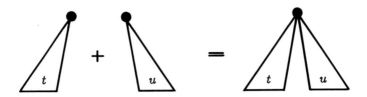

Figure A.2: *Possible nondeterministic transitions.*

NIL(nullary operation)
_____

NIL is the Υ •

+ (binary operation)
_____

$$+ \;\in\; \Upsilon_{R_1 \times E_1} \times \Upsilon_{R_2 \times E_2} \;\rightarrow\; \Upsilon_{R \times E}$$

where $R = (R_1 \cup R_2)$ and $E = (E_1 \cup E_2)$

$\underline{\alpha \ (\text{a } \omega\text{-ary operation})}$

α takes a set of members of $\Upsilon_{R \times E}$ indexed by the communications $k_0, k_1, \ldots,$ and produces a member of $\Upsilon_{R \times (E \cup acq(k_i))}$ for the $k_i\underline{\text{th}}$ member. This operation adds some new communication targeted to a given receptionist to the set of pending tasks; see Fig A.3. Let $K = \{k_0, k_1, \ldots\}$, then

$$\alpha \in (K \to \Upsilon_{R \times E}) \ \to \ \Upsilon_{R \times (E \cup acq(k_i))}$$

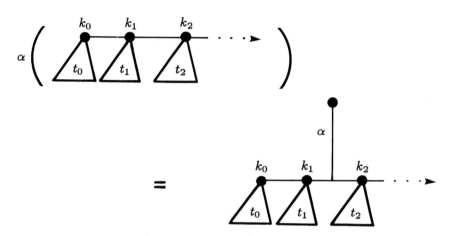

Figure A.3: *Possible new communications accepted by a given receptionist.*

$\underline{\overline{\alpha} \ (\text{a family of unary operations})}$

$$\forall k \ \overline{\alpha}(k) \ \in \ \Upsilon_{R \times E} \to \Upsilon_{(R \cup acq(k)) \times E}$$

$\overline{\alpha}(k)$ represents the fact that the communication k has been accepted by an external actor with the mail address α. See Fig A.4.

$\underline{\varrho \ (\text{a unary operation})}$

$$\varrho \in \Upsilon_{R \times E} \to \Upsilon_{R \times E}$$

ϱ represents an internal transition, i.e. the acceptance of a communication by an actor within the configuration.

The $+$ operation represents nondeterminism in the possible configurations a system may evolve to; specifically $t_1 + t_2$ simply means that we may

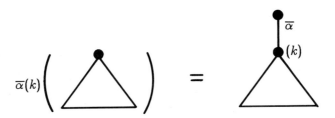

Figure A.4: *Acceptance of a communication by an external actor.*

be in the tree t_1 or in the tree t_2. The rest of the operations are straightforward and correspond to their description in the introduction. The trees differ from the transitions model of Chapter 5 in that they represent computation in an open system: It is possible to send a communication from the outside to a receptionist (the potential transitions are included to account for this fact). However configurations contain all the information necessary to map them into the trees and, furthermore, we can commute the diagram of the composition maps in configurations and Υ's.

The mechanics of how Υ's are built will become clearer with the composition operation. Composition will allow us to combine acceptance of communications sent to the receptionists (positive label bindings) in one tree with acceptance by the corresponding external actors (negative label bindings) in a different tree to create an internal action of the composite. We now provide three operations on Υ's, namely, (concurrent) composition, restriction, and relabeling.

Composition

Composition, $\parallel$, is a binary operation on Υ's such that:

$$\parallel \; \in \; \Upsilon_{R_1 \times E_1} \times \Upsilon_{R_2 \times E_2} \;\; \rightarrow \;\; \Upsilon_{R \times E}$$

where $R = (R_1 \cup R_2)$, $E = (E_1 - R_2) \cup (E_2 - R_1)$ and $(R_1 \cap R_2) = \emptyset$. Let $t \in \Upsilon_{R_1 \times E_1}$ and $u \in \Upsilon_{R_2 \times E_2}$, then $t \parallel u$ has the following branches:

(i) For each branch of t representing a communication from the outside to a receptionist (i.e., for the branches with the positive labels), there is a branch which represents the input followed by the composition with u of each of the trees it dominates. This branch reflects the fact that communications may be received by receptionists in t before any other actions take place. *Mutatis mutandis* for the receptionist of u.

(ii) For each branch of t representing an internal transition, there is a branch corresponding to the internal transition followed by the composition with u of the tree it dominates. This simply says that the internal action could happen before any of the effects of composition happen. *Mutatis mutandis* for branches of u.

(iii) For each branch of t representing a communication to an external actor β there are two possibilities. If $\beta \notin R_2$ then there is simply a equivalent branch followed by the composition with u of the tree it dominates. Otherwise, for each branch of u representing a communication from the outside to the receptionist β, there is an internal action followed by the composition of the tree in u which follows accepting the given communication and the tree the "output" branch dominates. The acceptance has been internalized because of the composition. *Mutatis mutandis* for "output" branches of u.

The composition operator preserves arrival order nondeterminism since it simply represents the interleaving of all the possibilities.

Restriction

The *restriction* operation, $\backslash$, removes a receptionist from a system. The result is that the mail address removed is no longer available for composition with other trees. However, if the corresponding actor was involved in accepting any communications from actors within the configuration, then these transitions are unaffected. One obviously cannot remove internal actions since they are not "guarded" by the mail address. Formally,

$$\backslash \alpha \in \Upsilon_{R \times E} \to \Upsilon_{(R - \{\alpha\}) \times E}$$

Relabeling

Given a map from mail addresses to mail addresses, this operator changes both the positive and negative bindings associated with each. It is unary operator. Note that in an actor system, $R \cap E = \emptyset$, therefore positive and negative versions of the same label can not co-exist in the same Υ.

We skip the straight-forward recursive definitions of restriction and relabeling.

The algebra now behaves like the algebra of CTs; in particular, the same definitions of strong equivalence and observation equivalence can be used. Observation equivalence on Υ's provides an intuitively abstract description of actor systems and retains the right amount of information. We refer to [Milner 1980] for details.

An interesting, and not too difficult, exercise is to draw sufficient fragments of the Υ's for the two systems S_1 and S_2 used in discussion of the Brock-Ackerman anomaly (Section 7.3). These Υ's are indeed not observation equivalent.

One remark may be pertinent, if peripheral, here. Milner has shown that observation equivalence is a congruence relation for all operations except the "+" operator. The counter-example which shows that observation equivalence is not a congruence relation uses the absorption property of the NIL tree under the + operation. The counter-example would not work if NIL had internal transitions to NIL. In any case, a congruence relation can be defined in terms of observation equivalence.

Appendix B

A Glossary Of Actor Terms

acquaintance An actor α is an acquaintance of an actor β if β knows the mail address of α.

Act A minimal actor language which has a lisp-like syntax and incorporates linguistic constructs necessary for an actor language. Specifically, ACT provides the ability to branch on conditionals, concurrently compose actions, send communications, create actors, and specify replacement behavior.

Act3 A higher-level actor language, which provides linguistic support for automatic generation of customers and for delegation and inheritance.

actor A computational agent which has a mail address and a behavior. Actors communicate by message-passing and carry out their actions concurrently.

actor event diagram A pictorial representation of computation in actor systems. Collections of actor event diagrams augmented with pending events have been used to provide a domain for a fair fixed-point semantics for actors [Clinger 1981].

Apiary A multiprocessor network architecture to support actor systems. Each processor serves as a "worker" to carry out the computations for actors resident on the processor. In a coarse-grained architecture, large numbers of actors may time-share on a single processor. A fine-grained Apiary would use millions of processors. The Apiary supports migration of actors between processors to promote locality of reference and load balancing, distributed real-time garbage collection, and a mail system for routing communications.

arrival order nondeterminism Nondeterminism in the computation resulting from the fact that the order of arrival of communications is indeterminate. In particular, even when communications are sent from a given sender to given target, the order of arrival of communications may not correspond to the order in which they are sent.

asynchronous communication Communication is considered to be asynchronous when the sender does not have to wait for the recipient to be "ready" to accept a communication before the sender can send the communication.

asynchronous communication trees A pictorial representation of transitions in an actor system. The nodes of the tree are configurations and the branches correspond to the possible transitions from a given node.

behavior The behavior of an actor maps the incoming communication to a three tuple of tasks created, new actors created, and the replacement behavior.

communication The only mechanism by which actors may affect each other's behavior. The content of a message sent by an actor is called a communication.

concurrent composition Commands are said to be composed concurrently if the order of their execution is not predetermined. The execution of one command may precede the execution of another or their executions may overlap in time.

compositionality The property of some semantic models that the meaning of the composition of two systems is the composition of the meanings of the two systems. The actor model proposed in this book supports compositionality.

concurrency The potentially parallel execution of actions without a determinate predefined sequence for their actions.

customer A request communication contains the mail address of an actor called the customer to which a reply to the request is to be sent. Customers are dynamically created to carry out the rest of the computation, so that an actor sending a request to another actor can begin processing the next incoming communication without waiting for the subcomputations of the previous communication to complete.

continuations Continuations specify how the execution of the rest of the code should proceed after the evaluation of some expression. In actors, when the evaluation of some expression requires sending a communication to another actor, the continuation is implemented using a customer.

delayed evaluation An expression evaluation strategy in which computation proceeds without evaluating an expression until the value of the expression is actually needed. For example, an expression which is an argument to a function may not be evaluated until it is actually used in the function.

eager evaluation An expression evaluation strategy in which a computation proceeds concurrently with the evaluation of an expression which may be needed to complete the computation. For example, a function and its arguments may be evaluated concurrently.

event In the actor model, an event is the acceptance of a communication by an actor. In response to accepting a communication, an actor creates other actors, sends communications and specifies a replacement behavior; in an event based semantics these actions are considered a part of the event.

external actor An actor which is external to a configuration but whose mail address is known to some actor within the configuration. External actors are compiled into futures and allows one to dynamically compose different actor systems.

fairness A requirement that any concurrent action which is to be carried out is eventually carried out. In the actor model, the form of fairness assumed is a guarantee that all communications sent are received by the targets after an arbitrarily long delay.

future A future is an actor representing the value of a computation in progress. Futures can speed up a computation since they allow subcomputations using references to a value to proceed concurrently with the evaluation of an expression to compute the value. Communications sent to a future are queued until the value has been determined (see also eager evaluation).

global time A linear order on all events which is consistent both with the casual order of events and with the local times of different actors. Because of the laws of parallel processing, a unique global time cannot be defined in distributed concurrent systems such as actors.

guarantee of mail delivery The property of actor systems that any communication sent is eventually received.

history relation The mathematical relation between communications sent to the receptionists and those sent to external actors (i.e., the relation between inputs and outputs). A semantics based on history relations is insufficient to account for the behavior of nondeterministic concurrent systems. (Caution: The term is sometimes used more generally for any relation capturing the unfolding of events in an actor system).

internal transition A transition occurring as a result of executing a task within a configuration targeted to an actor also within the configuration.

lifeline The history of events occurring at a given actor. Actor event diagrams are made up of lifelines together with the causal links between their events.

laws of parallel processing A set of axioms constraining the the behavior of all concurrent systems. Such constraints stem from physical intuitions about causality and about locality of information within agents in a system.

local states function A function mapping the mail addresses of actors in a configuration to their current behavior.

mail address A virtual location by which an actor may be accessed. Each actor has a unique mail address which is invariant, although the behavior of an actor may change over time. Mail addresses generalize the notion of l-values in von Neumann architectures.

mail queue The queue of incoming communications sent to a given actor. The mail queue represents the arrival order of communications and provides the means to buffer communications until they are processed by the target actor.

mail system The underlying system providing routing and buffering of communications between actors.

observation equivalence An equivalence relation between two systems which is based only communications that are potentially observable. Two systems are equivalent if they have the same possible sequences of communications to and from the respective systems and the external world.

open systems Systems characterized by the ability to interact with agents outside it. Such agents may not be known to the system at the time they send communications to the system.

pipelining A mechanism by which different communications to the same target actor can be carried out concurrently. Because an actor can process the next communication in its mail queue as soon as it has computed its replacement behavior, some of the actions caused by different communications sent to a given actor may be carried out concurrently.

possible transition A configuration is said to have a possible transition to a second configuration if the latter can be obtained as a result of a task in the first configuration being processed by its target.

possibility relation The transitive closure of possibility transitions. The possibility relation between two configurations represents the fact that the first configuration may possibly evolve into the second.

built-in actors Actors whose behavior is predefined, in the underlying implementation language, in the firmware, or in the hardware. Examples of typical built-in actors are integers, booleans, etc. In response to processing a communication, actors send more communications until the message-passing is bottomed out in terms of built-in actors.

receptionist An actor to whom communications may be sent from outside the configuration to which it belongs. The set of receptionists evolves dynamically as the mail addresses of various actors may be communicated to actors outside the system.

reconfigurability The ability to change the network topology defined by the acquaintance links between actors. Actor systems are continually reconfigured since the mail address of an actor may be communicated to other actors.

relabeling A transformation which changes the mail addresses of actors and the tags of tasks in a configuration without changing the behavior of the system.

replacement behavior A behavior specified by an actor processing a communication which is used to process the next communication in the mail queue of the actor.

reply A communication sent in response to a request (see also customers).

request A communication asking for a response to be sent to a customer contained in the request.

restriction The removal of an actor from the set of receptionists because its mail address is no longer known outside the system.

Sal A minimal actor language with an algol-like syntax (see also *Act*).

serialized behavior An actor has serialized behavior if it is is history-sensitive, i.e. if it changes as a result of processing a communication.

subsequent transition The transition from one configuration to another which is the result of processing a finite number of communications including a given communication. The subsequent transition is used to model the unbounded nondeterminism resulting from the guarantee of mail delivery.

synchronous communication Communication between two actors requiring the sender to wait until the recipient acknowledges or otherwise responds to the communication before continuing with further processing. Synchronous communication in actors is implemented using customers.

tag A notation for uniquely identifying tasks in a configuration. Because of the restriction that no tag in a configuration be a prefix of any other tag or mail address in the configuration, a distributed scheme for locally generating tags for new tasks and mail addresses for new actors created as the system evolves can be specified.

target The mail address to which a communication is sent. Communication in actors is point to point between actors.

task A three tuple composed of a tag which uniquely identifies each task in a configuration, a target which is the mail address of an actor to which the communication is to be sent, and a communication.

transaction A transaction is the partial order of events between a given request and the response (reply or complaint) it generates. Since a request may result in other requests which must be responded to before a reply can be generated to the original request, transactions may be nested.

unbounded nondeterminism A system exhibits unbounded nondeterminism if for some fixed input it is guaranteed to send one of an infinite number of possible communications. Unbounded nondeterminism cannot be modelled by a finitely branching tree. In actor systems, unbounded nondeterminism results from the guarantee of mail delivery and is modelled using the subsequent transition.

unserialized behavior The behavior of an actor which does not change in response to any incoming communication. Mathematical functions transforming values have unserialized behaviors.

References

[Ackerman 1984] W. B. Ackerman. *Efficient Implementation of Applicative Languages*. LCS Tech Report 323, MIT, March 1984.

[Agerwala and Arvind 1982] T. Agerwala and Arvind. Data flow systems. *Computer*, 15(2), Feb 1982.

[Agha 1985] G. Agha. Semantic considerations in the actor paradigm of concurrent computation. In *Seminar on Concurrency*, pages 151–179, Springer-Verlag, 1985.

[Backus 1978] J. Backus. Can programming be liberated from the von neumann style? a functional style and its algebra of programs. *Communications of the ACM*, 21(8):613–641, August 1978.

[Baker and Hewitt 1977] H. Baker and C. Hewitt. The incremental garbage collection of processes. In *Conference Record of the Conference on AI and Programming Languages*, pages 55–59, ACM, Rochester, New York, August 1977.

[Brinch Hansen 1977] Per Brinch Hansen. *The Architecture of Concurrent Programs*. Prentice-Hall, Englewood Cliffs, N.J., 1977.

[Brock and Ackerman 1981] J.D. Brock and W.B. Ackerman. *Scenarios: A Model of Non-Determinate Computation*, pages 252–259. *Lecture Notes in Computer Science*, Springer-Verlag, 1981.

[Brock 1983] J. D. Brock. *A Formal Model of Non-determinate Dataflow Computation*. LCS Tech Report 309, MIT, Aug 1983.

[Brookes 1983] S.D. Brookes. *A Model For Communicating Sequential Processes*. Technical Report CMU-CS-83-149, Carnegie-Mellon, 1983.

[Clinger 1981] W. D. Clinger. *Foundations of Actor Semantics*. AI-TR-633, MIT Artificial Intelligence Laboratory, May 1981.

[Costa and Stirling 1984] G. Costa and C. Stirling. A fair calculus of communicating systems. In *Foundations of Computer Theory, LNCS*, Springer-Verlag, 1984.

[Dahl, Myhrhaug and Nygaard 1970] O. J. Dahl, B. Myhrhaug and K. Nygaard. *Simula Common Base Language*. Technical Report S-22, Norwegian Computing Center, October 1970.

[Date 1983] C.J. Date. *An Introduction to Database Systems*. Addison-Wesley, 1983.

[deBakker and Zucker 1982] J.W. de Bakker and J.I. Zucker. Processes and the denotational semantics of concurrency. *Information and Control*, (54):70–120, 1982.

[deBakker 1980] J.W. de Bakker. *Mathematical Theory of Program Correctness*. Prentice-Hall International, 1980.

[Dijkstra 1971] E. W. Dijkstra. Hierarchical ordering of sequential processes. *Acta Informatica*, 1:115–138, 1971.

[Dijkstra 1977] E. W. Dijkstra. *A Discipline of Programming*. Prentice-Hall, 1977.

[Feynman, Leighton and Sands 1965] R. Feynman, R. Leighton and M. Sands. *The Feynman Lectures on Physics*. Addison-Wesley, 1965.

[Gray 1980] J. Gray. *Experience with the System R Lock Manager*. Memo, IBM San Jose Research Laboratory, 1980.

[Gurd, Kirkham and Watson 1985] J.R. Gurd, C.C. Kirkham and I. Watson. The manchester prototype dataflow computer. *Communications of the ACM*, 28(1):34–52, January 1985.

[Harel 1979] D. Harel. *First-Order Dynamic Logic*. Volume 68 of *Lecture Notes in Computer Science*, Springer-Verlag, 1979.

[Henderson 1980] P. Henderson. *Functional Programming: Applications and Implementation*. Prentice-Hall International, 1980.

[Hewitt and Atkinson 1977] C. Hewitt and R. Atkinson. Synchronization in actor systems. In *Proceedings of Conference on Principles of Programming Languages*, pages 267–280, January 1977.

[Hewitt and Baker 1977a] C. Hewitt and H. Baker. Laws for communicating parallel processes. In *1977 IFIP Congress Proceedings*, pages 987–992, IFIP, August 1977.

[Hewitt and Baker 1977b] C.E. Hewitt and H. Baker. Actors and continuous functionals. In Erich J. Neuhold, editor, *Proceedings IFIP Working Conference on Formal Description of Programming Concepts*, pages 367–387, IFIP, August 1977.

[Hewitt and deJong 1983] C. Hewitt and P. de Jong. Analyzing the roles of descriptions and actions in open systems. In *Proceedings of the National Conference on Artificial Intelligence*, AAAI, August 1983.

[Hewitt, et al 1985] C. Hewitt, T. Reinhardt, G. Agha and G. Attardi. Linguistic support of serializers for shared resources. In *Seminar on Concurrency*, pages 330–359, Springer-Verlag, 1985.

[Hewitt 1977] C.E. Hewitt. Viewing control structures as patterns of passing messages. *Journal of Artificial Intelligence*, 8-3:323–364, June 1977.

[Hewitt 1980] C.E. Hewitt. Apiary multiprocessor architecture knowledge system. In P.C. Treleaven, editor, *Proceedings of the Joint SRC/University of Newcastle upon Tyne Workshop on VLSI, Machine Architecture, and Very High Level Languages*, pages 67–69, University of Newcastle upon Tyne Computing Laboratory Technical Report, October 1980.

[Hoare 1978] C. A. R. Hoare. Communicating sequential processes. *CACM*, 21(8):666–677, August 1978.

[Holland 1975] J.H. Holland. *Adaptation in Natural and Artificial Systems*. U. of Michigan Press, 1975.

[Kahn and MacQueen 1978] K. Kahn and D. MacQueen. Coroutines and networks of parallel processes. In *Information Processing 77: Proceedings of the IFIP Congress, IFIP*, pages 993–998, Academic Press, 1978.

[Keller 1977] R.M. Keller. Denotational models for parallel programs with indeterminate operators. In *Proceedings of the IFIP Working Conference on Formal Description of Programming Concepts*, IFIP, August 1977.

[King and Collmeyer 1973] P. King and A. Collmeyer. Database sharing: an efficient mechanism for supporting concurrent processes. In *Proceedings of NCC*, 1973.

[Lynch and Fischer 1981] N. Lynch and J. Fischer. On describing behavior and implementation of distributed systems. *Theoret. Comp. Science*, 13(1), 1981.

[Manthey and Moret 1983] M. Manthey and B. Moret. The computational metaphor and quantum physics. *CACM*, February 1983.

[McCarthy 1959] John McCarthy. *Recursive Functions of Symbolic Expressions and their Computation by Machine*. Memo 8, MIT, March 1959.

[Mead and Conway 1980] C. Mead and L. Conway. *Introduction to VLSI Systems*. Addison-Wesley, Reading, MA, 1980.

[Meijer and Peeters 1982] A. Meijer and P. Peeters. *Computer Network Architectures*. Computers Science Press, 1982.

[Milner 1980] R. Milner. *A Calculus of Communicating Systems.* Volume 92 of *Lecture Notes in Computer Science,* Springer-Verlag, 1980.

[Plotkin 1971] G.D. Plotkin. *Assigning and Evaluating in Program Schemata.* Dept. of Machine Intelligence and Perception Memo MIP-R-86, University of Edinburgh, March 1971.

[Pnueli 1983] A. Pnueli. On the extremely fair treatment of probabilistic algorithms. In *Proceedings of the Fifteenth Annual ACM Symposium on the Theory of Computing,* 1983.

[Scott 1972] D. S. Scott. Lattice theoretic models for various type-free calculi. In *Proceedings 4th International Congress in Logic, Methodology and the Philosophy of Science,* Bucharest, Hungary, 1972.

[Scott 1982] D. S. Scott. Domains for denotational semantics. In *ICALP-82,* Aarhus, Denmark, July 1982.

[Seitz 1985] C. Seitz. The cosmic cube. *Communications of the ACM,* 28(1):22–33, January 1985.

[Stoy 1977] Joseph E. Stoy. *Denotational Semantics: The Scott-Strachey Approach to Programming Language Theory.* The MIT Press, Cambridge, MA, 1977.

[Theriault 1983] D. Theriault. *Issues in the Design and Implementation of Act2.* Technical Report 728, MIT Artificial Intelligence Laboratory, June 1983.

[vanEmden and Filho 1982] M. H. van Emden and G. J. de Lucena Filho. Predicate logic as a language for parallel programming. In *Logic Programming,* Academic Press, 1982.

[vonNeumann 1958] J. von Neumann. *The Computer and the Brain.* Yale U. Press, New Haven, Conn., 1958.

[Weng 1975] K.-S. Weng. *Stream-Oriented Computation in Data Flow Schemas.* TM 68, MIT Laboratory For Computer Science, October 1975.

[Wirth 1972] N. Wirth. *The Programming Language Pascal.* Technical Report, Eidgenossiche Technische Hochschule Zurich, November 1972.

Index

The MIT Press, with Peter Denning as consulting editor, publishes computer science books in the following series:

ACM Doctoral Dissertation Award and Distinguished Dissertation Series

Artificial Intelligence, Patrick Winston and Michael Brady, editors

Charles Babbage Institute Reprint Series for the History of Computing, Martin Campbell-Kelly, editor

Computer Systems, Herb Schwetman, editor

Foundations of Computing, Michael Garey, editor

History of Computing, I. Bernard Cohen and William Aspray, editors

Information Systems, Michael Lesk, editor

Logic Programming, Ehud Shapiro, editor

The MIT Electrical Engineering and Computer Science Series

Scientific Computation, Dennis Gannon, editor